Heart Journey Accompanying Journal

Healing through Encounters with Jesus and Psychology

A study for women ready for wholeness

Heart Journey:

Healing through Encounters with Jesus and Psychology

Barbara Lowe

2023© by Barbara Lowe

BIBLE SCRIPTURES

Printed in the United States of America

Spirit Media and our logos are trademarks of Spirit Media

www.restorationmedia.co

9650 Strickland Rd STE 103-111

Raleigh, NC 27615

www.spiritmedia.us

1249 Kildaire Farm Rd STE 112

Cary, NC 27511

1 (888) 800-3744

Kindle Store › Kindle eBooks › Health, Fitness & Dieting
Books › Self-Help › Personal Transformation
Books › Health, Fitness & Dieting › Psychology & Counseling
Books › Christian Books & Bibles › Christian Living

Paperback ISBN: 978-1-961614-18-5
Hardback: 978-1-961614-20-8
Audiobook ISBN: 978-1-961614-21-5
eBook ISBN: 978-1-961614-19-2

Endorsements

In *Heart Journey*™, Dr. Barbara Lowe's expertise in trauma healing shines through as she skillfully guides women on a transformative journey of healing and restoration. This invaluable tool equips individuals to navigate the complexities of their past, offering them a path to deep healing and the restoration of their God-given purpose. This is a groundbreaking resource that weaves together the principles of the Christian faith and the science of trauma healing.

DR. TIM CLINTON
President, American Association of Christian Counselors

Because virtually everybody, including Christians, has had some kind of trauma in life, there is a great need for sound, Christian resources that explain simply how to get the healing people need. But this book is very special. It is so biblical, so trauma-informed, and so accessible – all in one – written by someone with years of experience working with trauma, it guides readers step-by-step into a comprehensive, yet extremely practical, Christian model of trauma healing.

ERIC L. JOHNSON, PH.D.
Professor of Christian Psychology, Houston Christian University

Amidst a vast sea of literature, *Heart Journey*™ stands out as a groundbreaking resource that offers a truly unique and transformative approach to personal growth, guiding individuals from soul pain to God-sized purpose. Dr. Lowe's remarkable understanding of the inner world and her ability to lead women on a journey of deep healing and renewal sets her apart in the field.

JON GORDON
15x Best-Selling Author of The One Truth and The Garden

Heart Journey™ is an exceptional and vital addition to the realms of ministry and psychology. It seamlessly blends a Christian worldview with the science of trauma healing, establishing a solid foundation that is both accessible and practical. I wholeheartedly endorse this book and journal to women within the body of

Christ, as it offers profound healing for the heart. Furthermore, I recommend it to my esteemed colleagues as an exemplar of the harmonious integration between our indigenous Christian psychology and the science of trauma healing.

HAROLD G. KOENIG, M.D.
Professor of Psychiatry and Behavioral Sciences
Associate Professor of Medicine
Duke University Medical Center, Durham, North Carolina
Adjunct Professor, Department of Medicine, King Abdulaziz University,
Jeddah, Saudi Arabia
Visiting Professor, Shiraz University of Medical Sciences, Shiraz, Iran
Editor-in-Chief, International Journal of Psychiatry in Medicine

Dr. Barbara has given us a powerful gift in *Heart Journey*™. Informed by her experience as a Christian minister and a clinical psychologist, and guided by principles from psychology and neuroscience, *Heart Journey*™ meets each of us at our place of need. Through her conversational tone, Dr. Barbara shares impactful stories, informative teaching, and practical guidance that can transform your life. This book reflects the power of integrating the truths of Scripture, encounters with Jesus, and evidence-based tools that can help each of us heal, grow, and thrive.

NII ADDY, PH.D.
Yale Neuroscientist, Professor, and Podcast Host

As a licensed psychologist and Christian minister, Dr. Barbara Lowe understands and affirms both that trauma and unmet psychological needs are widespread in our world and that we are beloved creatures of God, who desires our wholeness and flourishing. While not intended as a substitute for therapy, *Heart Journey*™ is filled to the brim with practical and grounded exercises that can help our hearts unburden from the weight of anxiety and inability to trust in ourselves or others, and to open to a life of freedom and secure rest in God's love. In this hopeful book, Dr. Lowe offers an encouraging pathway to spiritual and psychological restoration and healing.

WARREN KINGHORN, MD, THD
Associate Professor of Psychiatry, Duke University Medical Center
Esther Colliflower Associate Professor of the Practice of Pastoral and
Moral Theology, Duke Divinity School
Co-Director, Theology, Medicine, and Culture Initiative, Duke Divinity School

This book is a timely gift and a rich treasure to the Body of Christ at this time and era of the church and where we find ourselves placed in society today. We have had a huge value in our movement on leaders walking through regular heart healing to unlock the potential God has for them so this heart fruit can filter through a church community. The purpose is that the love of God will be manifested in all that we do in our churches, including how we love and engage our communities and bring the light of Christ to our cities.

Most of us arrive in adulthood with childhood scars, emotional wounds and traumas that limit us not only in our relationships with others but with God our Father Himself. Our own testimony of heart healing and transformation over more than two decades as church Pastors is proof of this, as we have engaged in different forms and models of heart healing and deliverance on a continuous basis.

We have seen the great need for not only psychological theories of transformation but Holy Spirit-inspired, Scripture-filled material that will be tools in the hands of thousands of church leaders, lay leaders, church members, and families placed across every sphere of culture.

We believe that as you deep dive into this book and journal, taking the hand of the Holy Spirit Himself, He wants to walk with you as you unlock the deep places of your heart so that you can become the person you are called to be living your best life in Him!

KATE AND DUNCAN SMITH
Senior Leaders of Catch the Fire Raleigh
Presidents of Catch the Fire World, a global movement of churches,
ministry and missions

Dr. Barbara's skills and giftedness in bringing together psychology, theology, and neuroscience are rare, if not unparalleled. Fortunately, we have a gift and a tool in *Heart Journey*™. Trauma and pain seem ubiquitous, but *Heart Journey*™ is an effective antidote.

Dr. Barbara personally and clinically knows that inner healing is not beyond reach. The all-wise God, who desires wholeness, often uses people who have been "through the valley of tears, only to make it a place of springs" (Psalm 84:6). I highly endorse my friend, Dr. Barbara Lowe, and encourage you to journey forward with her.

RON LEWIS
Bishop, King's Park churches
Every Nation NYC
Jordan Lewis Missions

Author, Miracles in Manhattan

In a world where women are yearning for healing, purpose, and restoration, Dr. Barbara Lowe's *Heart Journey*™ book and journal shines as an unyielding beacon of hope. As a woman deeply immersed in both business and ministry, I have had the privilege of witnessing firsthand the remarkable and transformative impact of Dr. Lowe's ministry as a speaker. Time and again, I have seen the profound effectiveness of the *Heart Journey*™ process in the lives of those around me. This extraordinary resource impeccably blends a Christian worldview with the science of trauma healing, providing women with a practical roadmap to embark on a deeply personal and fulfilling journey of inner healing. Without a doubt, this is a must-do study for anyone seeking true transformation.

Within the pages of the *Heart Journey*™ book and journal, Dr. Lowe masterfully integrates psychology with profound encounters with Jesus and the living Word of God. This groundbreaking approach fearlessly calls women to courageously confront their past, release the burdens that weigh them down, and embrace a future overflowing with purpose and meaning. Through the exploration of stability skills, resilience-building practices, narrative examination, and profound heart healing, readers are guided toward experiencing the life-altering power of forgiveness, surrender, and restoration. Dr. Lowe's teachings and insights, deeply rooted in her own life of authenticity and unwavering faith, bear witness to the profound impact of this resource.

If you are a woman yearning to heal the depths of your heart, unlock your true potential, and step into a life of profound significance, the *Heart Journey*™ book and journal are the perfect companions for your sacred journey. Discover the immense power that comes from integrating your faith with psychological healing, and embrace a future that is marked by profound wholeness, unshakable purpose, and a deeper connection with our beloved Savior. Prepare to be transformed as you embark on this extraordinary path toward true healing, restoration, and a life that shines with the radiance of God's love.

LYNETTE LEWIS
TEDx Speaker
Author
Business Consultant

Dr. Barbara has written with such great insight! You will be encouraged and inspired to begin your journey toward healing and wholeness. It is a compelling and spirit-filled study book that will make the broken heart thirsty for the healing you long for. It will guide you and quench your thirst with the knowledge imparted to you. Your innermost being will respond with courage as you encounter truth. The inner healing begins as you learn to pour out the pain of your past and find the freedom to live a future that is full, complete, and free indeed in Christ. The truth shared in this book has the power to break the yoke of bondage and set the captive free!

ANNE BEILER
Founder of Auntie Anne's Pretzels
Author and Speaker

In *Heart Journey*™, Dr. Barbara Lowe guides women on a much-needed journey in trauma healing and the wholeness available in Christ. The heartwork instructions are simple to follow with a lasting and profound impact. This book is a valuable tool for both individuals and clinicians, sharing relevant scientific processes alongside scriptural truths to offer a transformational journey to restore mind-body-spirit well-being.

DR. SAUNDRA DALTON-SMITH
Bestselling Author of Sacred Rest and Host of I Choose My Best Life

I am honored to wholeheartedly endorse Dr. Barbara Lowe's integrated *Heart Journey*™ book and journal. As the creator and co-leader of the SOZO inner healing method, I have great anticipation of the powerful impact this book and study guide will have on women of all ages. I am confident that this resource will continue to bring transformational breakthroughs to all who are willing to allow God to remodel and beautify their heart home. I have watched Dr. Barbara gather, empower, and bring whole heart healing to hundreds of women over the past five years I have known her. This book is not only written from a therapist who knows how to fix you but dually from a researched, educated, devoted believer who has allowed God to entirely remodel her own heart home. Roll up your sleeves, get your work clothes on, put your hands to the plow, and be amazed at how God will restore beauty from your life's ashes.

DAWNA DE SILVA
Bethel Sozo, Co-Leader
Author of Sozo: Saved, Healed, Delivered
Shifting Atmospheres
Atmospheres 101
Overcoming Fear
Prayers, Declarations, and Strategies
Warring with Wisdom

Often, the challenges we are faced with feel bigger than our blessings and potential. They call into question our peace and our place. Dr. Barbara Lowe's *Heart Journey*™ offers profound insight and practical tools providing the much-needed support that serves to strengthen the foundation our faith is built on. At different times in my life as a young woman of faith, I have longed for such a clear and impactful ministry. It brings me great joy to know that women the world over will now have this life changing place of healing to grow from. I strongly encourage anyone in need of emotional and spiritual wholeness to dive deeply into this phenomenal book. As I tip my hat to this extraordinary woman and this indispensable resource, I am reminded of this bit of Scripture, "Peace I leave you; my peace I give you. I do not give to you as the world gives. Do not let your hearts be troubled and do not be afraid." – John 14:27

LISA KIMMEY WINANS
Recording Artist
Actress
Speaker

Heart Journey™ is a beautifully woven synthesis bringing together clinical research with spiritual truths producing a profoundly transformative masterpiece. Dr. Barbara's clinical work and research provide a holistic perspective to honor body, soul, and spirit in a cohesive blend that fosters sustainable healing. The *Heart Journey*™ book and journal seamlessly walk the reader through a process that fosters past healing and empowers participants to live fullheartedly from their true selves into their life purpose. A true treasure that has exquisite value that will benefit everyone!

DR. SHANNAN CRAWFORD
Licensed Psychologist
Executive Coach

Speaker

When it comes to healing the matters of the heart, it is of utmost importance to seek guidance from one who has answered the call of Jesus—one who knows Jesus, one with heart-healing experience, one whose leadership can be trusted, one who has your best in mind. Dr. Barbara Lowe is that one. She is one I would trust with the matters of my own heart. You can get whole. Dr. Barbara will guide you to healing and wholeness in her deeply insightful and spiritually powerful new book and companion journal—*Heart Journey*™: Healing through Encounters with Jesus & Psychology and *Heart Journey Journal.*

DR. KIM MAAS
Founder/CEO Kim Maas Ministries
Author of Prophetic Community: God's Call For All to Minister in His
Gifts and The Way of the Kingdom: Seizing the Times For a Great Move of God

I am honored to offer my enthusiastic endorsement of Dr. Barbara Lowe's groundbreaking book, *Heart Journey*™. As an international speaker, consultant, published author, and Doctor of Theology specializing in Cultural Restoration and Leadership, I have had the privilege of witnessing firsthand the transformative power of Dr. Lowe's teachings. With her exceptional understanding of inner healing and trauma restoration, impeccably blended with a Christian worldview, Dr. Lowe's work in *Heart Journey*™ serves as a beacon of hope for women seeking healing, purpose, and restoration. Her masterful integration of profound encounters with Jesus, the living Word of God, with the principles of inner healing creates a life-altering experience that calls readers to courageously confront and heal from their past, embrace forgiveness, and step into a future overflowing with unshakable faith and profound significance. Prepare to be profoundly transformed as you embark on this extraordinary journey of inner healing guided by Dr. Lowe's expertise and unwavering commitment to empowering women to live lives of wholeness and God-breathed purpose.

DR. TRACEY STRAWBERRY
International Speaker, Consultant, and Trainer
Founder of Finding Your Way
Author: The Imperfect Marriage, Help for Those Who Think It's Over
Author: Clean Sober & Saved Christ-Centered Recovery Curriculums

Author Participant: The Invitation to Intimacy with God Devotional
Co-Author: Straw, Finding My Way (Biography of Darryl Strawberry)

In the current age of intense external pressures and unresolved traumas, the levels of confusion and anxiety among adults and children are alarming ... even within the Church! In The *Heart Journey*™, Dr. Barbara Lowe has made it possible for you to face the pain that triggers your anxieties. She offers practical tools to effectively apply the Word of God to whatever is driving you. Say goodbye to the empty rhetoric that has shamed you in the past and say hello to your freedom!

Brenda Crouch - Author, Speaker, TV Host

In my sixteen years of pastoring and supporting those with trauma, I haven't found a resource as comprehensive as the *Heart Journey*™ book and the accompanying *Heart Journey*™ *Journal*—the tools, exercises, and biblical truths Dr. Barbara Lowe-Suave has compiled will bring restoration, wholeness, purpose, and lifelong wellness to those who commit to the journey. In addition, participants will have intimate encounters with Jesus and deepen their relationship with Him and others. The *Heart Journey*™ Book and Journal are life-changing resources for individuals and small groups.

Verna Brown
Senior Pastor of Soul Harvest Worship Center
Writer
Speaker

Heart Journey™ is a comprehensive curriculum which actively addresses and provides practical solutions to the hurt, pain, and disappointments that victims of trauma hide in their hearts. This system is a blueprint of wholeness that was developed on a foundation of biblical principles intertwined with professional psychological insight. God is using Dr. Barbara in supernatural ways to provide healing and restoration to everyone. Her passion exudes from the pages of the book and accompanying journal, giving you practical steps throughout your journey of healing. It addresses your emotional, spiritual and physical recovery needs. I encourage both men and women to be bold enough to take the path of healing and restoration. You owe it to yourself to heal. In doing so, you will experience God's love in ways you never imagined, allowing you to accomplish what you've only dreamed of.

Valora Shaw-Cole
Senior Co-Pastor Contagious Church
Speaker
Author

Heart Journey™ is a game changer for the world. This book is a blueprint with scientific research that helps us better understand the intricacies of the heart and the biblical principles that can help you experience real transformative healing from past trauma. I recommend this book as a resource to guide you through your personal journey to freedom. Every believer should read this book and use it as a tool to help enhance their insight of the inner man and equip them to bring practical healing to the brokenhearted.

ANDY ARGUEZ
Senior Pastor of Supernatural Culture Church
International Speaker
Author
Senior Ambassador of Philcoin

Dr. Lowe has created an incredible resource for those trying to heal from a painful past and significant trauma. *The Heart Journey*™ focuses on critical aspects of people's pain that most traditional therapy can ignore altogether or only minimally address. At its foundation, this book and journal allow an intimate relationship with God and spiritual growth in Christ to lead the process of healing and recovery. It is a valuable resource for trauma survivors.

JENNIFER ELLERS, MA
Institute for Compassionate Care

I appreciate Dr. Barbara Lowe's ability to integrate Christian psychology, a Biblically-grounded approach to inner healing of the heart, and encounters with Jesus. *Heart Journey*™ will help many become unstuck and gain forward progress in their pursuit of living wholly!

ANA WERNER
Founder, President, Eagles Network
Author The Seer's Path

I have had the privilege of knowing Dr. Barbara Lowe, my dear friend and Kingdom co-laborer, for over twenty years. From our early days, it was evident to me that Dr. Barbara possessed a powerful blend of compassion for others, a thirst to understand the inner workings of the human psyche, and a hunger for the deeper elements of God. *Heart Journey*™ addresses the multifaceted aspects of trauma, taking into account the emotional, psychological, and spiritual dimensions that intertwine deep within the human soul. Dr. Barbara draws upon her expertise in psychology and her passion for ministry to guide readers on a transformative path toward wholeness. I am confident, whether you are a person of faith or not, the wisdom shared in these pages will resonate with your deepest longing for healing and restoration. It is both an honor and a privilege to endorse *Heart Journey*™ for anyone seeking to understand the profound impact of trauma upon one's life, while also desiring to embark on a journey of healing. This book is indeed a gift!

DEBORAH KIRBY
Founder of Joy In The Morning Ministries, Inc.
Author, Beyond the Greenhouse
Executive Director, Greenleaf Psychological and Support Services
Beloved friend and Kingdom co-laborer of Dr. Barbara's Now and Into Eternity

As a minister, I have spent many years investing in the hearts of women. I have been through many different inner healing ministries, and while this book incorporates many such teachings, Dr. Barbara's *Heart Journey*™ is the most comprehensive inner healing method that I have ever experienced. What distinguishes this book is that it incorporates psychology, biblically-based faith tools, and encounters with Jesus to bring healing to the entire person: body, soul, and spirit. I wholeheartedly believe this is a tool for the body of Christ to be healed so that we can be whole vessels that can contain the precious oil of the Holy Spirit and not spill it out through all of our wounds and triggers. The resources in this book work even when nothing else has. This book and journal have changed my life, my marriage, and my family. *Heart Journey*™ has healed my heart, brought stability to my soul, and helped my behavior to better reflect my Lord and Savior. This is the case not just for me but for many friends who have gone on this heart transformation journey with me. It is time for the women of God to arise, repair our vessels, and fill up our oil lamps to be ready for our heavenly bridegroom to come for His glorious bride.

ASHLEY ODVODY
Mom of Three, Entrepreneur, AACC Certified Mental Health Coach, and Minister

Dr. Barbara is a true gem, both brilliant and compassionate. She is a lover of God, people, and knowledge. You get to benefit from her years of diligent study and her integration of psychology and ministry experience through her powerful, new book. She is no stranger to trauma, but she is also no stranger to overcoming insurmountable obstacles. Let Dr. Barbara guide you to the healing you are longing for through the *Heart Journey*™ book and journal.

ADRIENNE COOLEY
Author of the book series Happy ANYWAY, Love ANYWAY, & Believe ANYWAY;
Speaker, Senior Co-Pastor of HARVESTMobile.com

Disclaimer

I am Dr. Barbara Lowe, Ordained Minister, Licensed Psychologist, Master ART Therapist, Board Certified Life Coach, and Somatic Experiencing Practitioner. I come to you as a Christian Minister, not as a psychologist, as I write solely from an indigenous Christian perspective in this book. In my psychological practice, I always honor and work within the worldviews of my clients. However, as a ministry project, I am presenting this study from a Christian perspective. Of course, there is plenty of room for scientific psychology in a faith-filled Christian life, and I do from time to time refer to standard psychological principles and tools that are available to us all as we heal from trauma.

Please note that all the characters and stories depicted within are entirely fictional, except for Deborah (alias), who consented for the me, the author, to share her experiences following the *Heart Journey*™ Method.

This book does not feature any representation of clients from my psychotherapy practice or clinical work.

It is important to emphasize that this book is not intended to be a substitute for therapy. You, as the reader, should not consider yourself as a clinical or coaching client of me, the author, and should always seek guidance from s licensed healthcare provider regarding any health or mental health concerns. This book is intended solely for informational, educational, and Christian edification purposes and should not be used as a replacement for medical or mental health treatment. I have taken care to ensure the book does not contain content that might be overly triggering. However, as this book integrates Christian faith tools, encounters with the Lord, and self-employed psychology tools for inner healing and encounters with Jesus, some material may be triggering. As the reader, you are encouraged to self-monitor and use the skills taught in the first three chapters to self-regulate and reach a solid point of emotional safety. If, at any point, you feel unsafe or need immediate help, you should contact 911.

The book is dedicated to the hundreds of millions of Christians around the world who face severe persecution, terrorization, imprisonment, and martyrdom due to their faith today.[1]

I would like to express my gratitude to ChatGPT, an AI language model developed by OpenAI, for its invaluable help in editing and refining sections of this book. ChatGPT's insightful suggestions and improvements greatly contributed to the final quality of the manuscript.

A Note about Language

Although this book is written for women, it is my sincere hope that any person who would like to engage with this content would feel comfortable doing so.

Acknowledgements

I am deeply grateful for the remarkable contributions of Dr. Harold Koenig, Dr. Eric Johnson, Dr. Joshua Knabb, and numerous other pioneers in the field of healing the soul from an indigenous Christian Psychology perspective. Their groundbreaking contributions have paved the way for the profound healing journey within the *Heart Journey*™ framework. In addition, the faith integrative work by Drs. Henry Cloud and John Townsend has been invaluable.

Additionally, I owe a tremendous debt of gratitude to: Dr. Peter Levine, Dr. David Burns, Dr. Marsha Linehan, Dr. Richard Schwartz, Dr. John Bowlby, Dr. Mary Ainsworth, Dr. Stephen Hayes, Dr. Stephen Porges, Drs. John and Julie Gottman, Dr. Sue Johnson, Dr. Bessel Vander Kolk, Dr. Erik Erikson, Dr. Fritz Perls, Dr. Laura Perls, Dr. Daniel Wegner, Dr. Melanie Klein, Dr. Diana Baumrind, Dr. Barbara Fredrickson, Francine Shapiro, Dr. Mark McMinn, Bruce Ecker, Dr. Terrance Real, Dr. Dianne Poole Heller, Dr Heather Gingrich, Dr. Saundra Daulton Smith, Dr. Thomas Chess, and Dr. Alexander Thomas, along with countless other trailblazers who have spearheaded our understanding and healing of the mind, emotions, nervous system, and relationships. Your invaluable insights and advancements have laid many of the foundations for the transformative path of healing found within the *Heart Journey*™. *Heart Journey*™ builds upon your fundamental work.

I extend my gratitude to Dr. William R. Miller and Dr. Harold D. Delaney for their work as editors on Judeo-Christian Perspectives on Psychology: Human Nature, Motivation, and Change, published by the American Psychological Association (APA).[2] Thank you, Drs. Miller and Delaney, for your efforts in bringing together a work that explores elements of the Christian worldview and psychology that have been relevant for billions of people for millennia. I also express my appreciation to the APA for publishing this valuable contribution.

Thank you to Dr. Thema Bryant, 2023 APA president, for working for "psychology for the people," for acknowledging that your identities and roles as minister and psychologist can coexist, and for your efforts in breaking down prejudice toward the science of psychology in the Christian church. Thank you, "Dr. Thema", also for sharing your trauma story freely and publicly.[3]

Furthermore, I would like to express my heartfelt gratitude to my pastor, Bishop Ron Lewis, for his unwavering spiritual guidance and support on all matters, including the birth of my ministry. Your wisdom and counsel have been instrumental in shaping the spiritual foundations regarding the *Heart Journey*™ framework and my ministry efforts. Thank you for your steadfast presence and encouragement throughout this journey. Additionally, I would like to extend my sincere appreciation to Lynette Lewis, the author, speaker, and wife of Bishop Ron Lewis, for her unwavering support and encouragement throughout this process. Your presence, encouragement, and admonishments have been invaluable, and I am grateful for your contributions to the spiritual crossing of the *Heart Journey*™ framework. Moreover, I would like to thank Pastors Reggie and Bomi Roberson for their faithful insights regarding ministry direction. To all of you, thank you for your unwavering support and dedication.

I acknowledge the foundational publications and methodologies created by Dr. Karl Lehman and Dawna DeSilva, as well as in the domain of Christian inner healing.

I would like to extend special appreciations to Dr. Tonya Armstrong for her sagacious guidance on the ethical considerations pertaining to ministry and psychology throughout the years.

Additionally, the legal advice provided by Steve Shaber, Esq., John Swallow, Former State Attorney General, and Christy Compagnone, Esq., regarding the law pertaining to religious liberty, ministry, and the practice of psychology, has been incredibly beneficial.

Furthermore, I would like to express my appreciation to OpenAI, the developers of ChatGPT, an AI language model, for their invaluable assistance in editing and refining language for significant sections of this book. The insightful suggestions and improvements provided by ChatGPT have significantly enhanced the overall quality of the *Heart Journey*™ book and journal manuscripts. In particular, I would like to extend my gratitude to ChatGPT for its invaluable assistance in refining language, providing editing suggestions, and aiding in the search for relevant Bible sources. ChatGPT's contribution has been instrumental in ensuring the accuracy and authenticity of the *Heart Journey*™ book and journal.

Thank you to Elizabeth Charlé and Kevin White for your invaluable assistance in editing and publishing this work. Your expertise and dedication have greatly contributed to its quality and success.

Thank you to the many content experts in faith, inner healing, and/or psychology who endorsed this work. I deeply appreciate each of you. I am profoundly honored that you took the time to recommend *Heart Journey*™.

Moreover, I want to sincerely thank Ashley Odvody, Ugonna Ukwu, Pastor Verna Brown, Dr. Steve Greene, Dawna De Silva, Nancy Nelson, Elizabeth Johnson, and Deborah Kirby for their incredible support as I developed and wrote *Heart Journey*™.

Lastly, but also primarily, I would like to thank my beloved life-gift, my husband and pastor, Tim Sauvé, for all the spiritual formation and encouragement you have lavishly poured into me for decades. You are a large part of who I am becoming, and I thank you with gratitude that is beyond words.

Introduction to *Heart Journey*™ Study Tools

Heart Journey™ is a comprehensive book designed to guide us through a transformative process of heart healing and restoration. It provides a roadmap for those seeking emotional healing, inner peace, and a deeper connection with God.

Within the pages of *Heart Journey*™, you will discover a step-by-step process that will move you through stabilizing emotions and the nervous system, to healing unmet needs and traumas, to launching into life's purpose. It addresses various aspects of the heart including past hurts, unmet needs, traumas, nervous system response, parts of self, resentments, fears, shame, and self-judgment. Through engaging exercises and encounters with Jesus, you will be invited to delve into your own story, identify areas of brokenness, and open yourself up to healing encounters with the Lord.

But the journey is not complete with this book alone. The *Heart Journey*™ Journal provides a necessary companion resource that will allow you to apply the heart healing process in a more personal and interactive way. The journal is a required complement to the book by providing all the Heartwork exercises and activities that will actually facilitate the heart restoration you seek.

One of the unique features of the *Heart Journey*™ Journal is the inclusion of scripted activities that serve as healing meditations with Jesus. These activities are designed to bring you into encounters with Jesus and facilitate a deepening relationship with Him. By engaging with these scripted activities, you can experience transformative moments of connection, healing, and restoration.

To enhance the experience further, both the *Heart Journey*™ book and the *Heart Journey*™ Journal offer audio versions of the scripted activities. You can simply activate the QR code provided in the book or journal and submit your best email to access the audio content. This feature allows you to engage in guided Christian meditations and reflections, immersing yourself in the healing presence of Jesus through the power of sound.

Whether you choose to embark on the *Heart Journey*™ individually or as part of a group study, the combination of the book and journal offers a comprehensive and transformative experience. It is an invitation to journey deep into the recesses of the heart, encounter God's healing love, and emerge with a renewed sense of purpose, freedom, confidence, peace, and joy.

Heart Journey™ is not just a book or journal; it is a transformative voyage that will empower you to embrace healing, amalgamate with the heart of God, and experience the fullness of purpose for which you were created.

The *Heart Journey*™ study is a powerful resource; however, as noted above, it is important to recognize that reading alone is not enough. To experience true transformation and healing, it is vital to actively engage in the work presented in the *Heart Journey*™ *Journal*.

In the biblical story of the healing at Bethesda, we encounter a man who had been crippled for thirty-eight years. He found himself among many others who waited for healing by the pool. When Jesus saw him, he asked a profound question: "Do you truly long to be well?" This question challenges us to examine our own hearts and desires for healing and restoration.

Similarly, in our journey toward healing and wholeness, Jesus is there to meet us, but we, too, have a part to play. Just as the man had to respond to Jesus' command to "Stand up! Pick up your sleeping mat and walk," we are called to act in our own lives.

By actively participating in the Heartwork exercises in your *Heart Journey*™ *Journal*, you are responding to God's Word and opening yourself up to His healing touch. It is through this intentional engagement that the flow of healing can reach and transform your heart home.

Let Deborah[4] serve as our primary example in this study. She wholeheartedly embraced the work in her *Heart Journey*™ *Journal*, moving from a place where daily heart pain immobilized her to a life full of purpose and a river of living water flowing through her. Her commitment to the process brought about significant transformation and freedom.

Just like the man at the pool of Bethesda, we may have felt stuck, defeated, and unable to experience the healing we long for. But as we pick up our "mat" of past hurts, resentments, and brokenness, and actively engage in the *Heart Journey*™ process, we position ourselves to encounter the healing power of Jesus.

Similarly, in our journey toward healing and wholeness, Jesus is there to meet us, but we, too, have a part to play. It is important to remember the wisdom shared in James 2:17, which states that "faith without works is dead." Just as the man at the pool of Bethesda had faith that healing was possible, he also had to respond to Jesus' command and take action.

In our own lives, faith is not merely a passive belief, but an active force that requires us to step out in obedience and engage in the work that leads to transformation. Just like the man had to respond to Jesus' command to "Stand up! Pick up your sleeping mat and walk," we are called to take intentional steps forward in our healing journey.

The *Heart Journey*™ *Journal* (sold separately from the study) provides us with the tools and exercises necessary to actively participate in our own healing. It prompts us to reflect, to encounter Jesus's healing in our places of pain, to confront our resentments and fears, to forgive ourselves and others, and to surrender our burdens to God.

By aligning our faith with action, we open ourselves up to the transformative power of God. As we pick up our "mat" of past hurts and brokenness and actively engage in the Heartwork process, we follow Jesus into healing and restoration. It is through our willingness to put in the work that we can experience the miraculous transformation God desires for us.

So, as you embark on this journey of healing and growth, remember that your faith in God's healing power must be accompanied by action. Respond to His invitation, embrace the exercises in the *Heart Journey*™ *Journal*, and trust that as you take intentional steps forward, God will meet you in the process and bring about the healing and wholeness you seek.

I love you, I believe in you, I am with you, and even more, so is He!

Love,

Dr. Barbara

P.S. For those who have completed your initial journey with the Heart Journey™ *Study and Journal and desire to dive even deeper into the heart healing process, it is highly recommended to consider purchasing a second journal. Many women have found that going through the Heart Journey*™ *a second time can be a powerful continuation of healing and growth.*

Heart Journey™ Self-Assessment

And do not be conformed to this world, but be transformed by the renewing of your mind, that you may prove what is that good and acceptable and perfect will of God.

Romans 12:2 (NKJV)

In the same way we assess repairs to be made on a home, we must take an objective self-inspection of our heart. To get started on your *Heart Journey*™, complete the Assessment, Individual Heartwork - Reflection below.

INDIVIDUAL HEARTWORK REFLECTION—GETTING STARTED.

To get an idea of where your heart is now, journal below on how you are feeling.

1. How do you feel about starting on this journey? Excited? Nervous? Scared?

2. What do you believe is under this feeling?

3. What do you hope will come out of this study? Be a better mom, wife, or friend? Feel more like "yourself"? What is your goal?

4. What is the Lord whispering to you in this moment about your journey? Sit before Him and listen to what your spiritual ears hear Him saying about your Heart Journey™ and write it below (John 10:27).

INDIVIDUAL HEARTWORK – HEART INSPECTION

1. Describe what a whole heart would look and feel like.

2. On a scale of one to ten, how "whole" do you think your heart is right now?

3. What room or rooms in your heart (areas of your life) do you feel like need renovation?

4. Which rooms are in good shape?

5. Are there areas of your heart home where you have not wanted to look and just pushed them aside?

6. What area or areas of your heart do you feel need immediate repair for you to function?

7. What positive coping skills do you already use?

8. Describe how you use your relationship with the Lord to cope or soothe your soul.

9. Ask the Lord how He wants to soothe your soul, then sit and listen. Write what He says below.

HEART GROUP DISCUSSION — TIME TO SHARE.

Find a trusted friend or attend your Heart Journey™ small group, and take time to share about your "heart condition" and coping skills. As we encourage one another, let us pray together.

LET US PRAY.

Heavenly Father,

We come before You with broken hearts, in need of repair. Yet we know repairs do not just happen through our own meager attempts, but by Your transformative power. And that comes through Jesus' victory over death through the cross and resurrection, and by allowing You to renew our minds.

Lord, we come to You with open hearts. Open our eyes that we may see and our ears that we may hear which areas of our hearts need restoration. And we choose to yield our hearts to You for repair, trusting in Your perfect, divine plan.

In Jesus' name, Amen.

Notes for Small Group Facilitators

I am so grateful you have responded positively to the calling of facilitating a *Heart Journey*™ small group. I pray that your group experiences many healing encounters through Jesus' powerful love on this journey. To help make the most of this heart restoration process, following are some suggestions, but please feel free to tailor specific details according to your group's needs.

This book and journal presents a significant amount of material and includes many activities and opportunities for reflection and discussion. Please feel free to take your time working through the process. I suggest working through the journey with your group at the pace of one chapter every two weeks. Each chapter includes teaching, activities, supporting Scriptures, prayer, and questions for individual reflection and group discussion. To allow time for all of these activities, you will need at least two weekly meetings for each chapter. Then, if you need more time, please feel free to modify the timetable as necessary.

As you go through this material, please remind the individuals in your group that safety and security is a priority. Healing from emotional wounds can be overwhelming if the process moves too fast; titration and pacing are necessary. If, at any time someone does not feel safe, please encourage them to talk to a professional and not move forward with additional Heartwork until they are ready. Safety is always your priority. In the rare instance that a life-threatening situation occurs, call 911 immediately.

During the journey, encourage your group members to make intimate, heart-to-heart connections within your group so they can encourage and pray for one another in between weekly meetings. Facilitate belonging and the felt sense of "every voice matters."

Those who have been through much trauma may tend to dominate the group with sharing traumas. Keep the sharing balanced among members. Make sure to keep the overall focus more on Jesus rather than the work of the enemy, while encouraging appropriate sharing of the "real." If the group does not meet enough needs for a participant, recommend help from a professional licensed psychotherapist along with the small group. This study is not a substitute for professional mental health care.

Your role is to facilitate discussion, belonging, support, and prayer, and to share your experience, strength, and hope in Jesus. Never succumb to a pressure to provide counseling, but refer to licensed professional mental health therapists.

Speaking God's Word

In Ephesians 6:17, the sword of the Spirit is listed as the Word of God. As the only offensive weapon in God's armor, Scripture serves as a powerful tool to which we have direct and constant access. God loves when we confess His word out loud and promises us that speaking His word will accomplish His desires and purpose for our lives.

The Word of God that I speak from my mouth will not return to Him empty, but will accomplish what He desires and achieve the purpose for which He sent it to me.

Isaiah 55:11 (NIV)

This Book of the Law shall not depart out of my mouth, but I shall meditate on it day and night, that I may observe and do according to all that is written in it. For then the Lord shall make my way prosperous, and then I shall deal wisely and have good success.

Joshua 1:8 (AMP)

The Lord watches over His word to perform it.

Jeremiah 1:12 (AMP)

As you just read in the above Scriptures, God takes the speaking of His words seriously. Beloved, He actually watches over it to ensure it is carried through. The Word of God gives us more than 3,500 promises that cover the gamut of topics we can claim for our daily living. As we study each chapter, it is important to pray the Word of God out loud, especially as it pertains to each section's topic. To facilitate a powerful release of your faith, I have included three Scriptures for each chapter. Beloved, use these as strong offensive weapons to overcome the enemy while on your Heart Journey™. Mediate on His living and active Word (Hebrews 4:12), and speak it daily out loud. His word will change you and your circumstances!

Table of Contents

Chapter

ONE

RESTORING MY HEART

The Spirit of the Sovereign Lord is on me, because the Lord has anointed me to proclaim good news to the poor. He has sent me to bind up the brokenhearted, to proclaim freedom for the captives and release from darkness for the prisoners.

Isaiah 61:1 (NIV)

SUPPLIES

For this chapter's Heartwork, you will need a pen or pencil and your *Heart Journey*™ *Journal.*

YOUR STORY

Beloved, what is your story? Does your story resemble Tonya's or Ashley's? Maybe yours is similar to Deborah's, or maybe you have one that is a combination of all three. Take some time now to reflect and journal on your story. It is healing to write and to share your story.

 **Heart** Journey

INDIVIDUAL HEARTWORK – YOUR STORY

Reflect on your story, and journal below.

1. What was your upbringing like?

2. What was positive and what was negative?

3. How did these experiences shape your inner life?

INDIVIDUAL HEARTWORK – YOUR NEEDS

Take a moment to reflect on the following questions and jot down your responses. You can revisit them later to gauge the progress you and Jesus have made in reconstructing the various areas of your heart.

1. As you reflect on basic needs we each have, what basic needs were well-met during your childhood?

2. How did having those needs met contribute to your well-being as you grew into an adult?

3. Which basic needs were not met?

4. What impact did not having these basic needs met have on you as you grew into an adult?

5. In reflection, how did you see God working in your life when basic needs were unmet?

6. Sit before the Lord and ask Him to share with you how He sees your heart home. Then write down the loving truth your Father speaks to you.

HEART GROUP DISCUSSION – TIME TO SHARE.

Being vulnerable and real with safe others is part of your healing, but if you do not yet feel comfortable sharing with your small group or a trusted friend or family member, there is no pressure to do so. Building strong relationships takes time. As you begin this journey, each of you likely has a myriad of emotions waiting to be processed, as well as specific outcomes you hope will come out of your heart restoration. Take some time to share with each other (if you feel comfortable) your responses to the following questions:

1. What prompted you to consider taking this Heart Journey™?

2. Have you ever delved into heart matters before starting this journey? If so, take time to share.

3. Do you have any expectations for your journey? If so, what are they? If not, why do you think that is the case?

4. Do you have a favorite Scripture Jesus has placed on your heart regarding this journey? If so, how has this Scripture encouraged you up to this point?

5. Take time to share with your group (if you feel comfortable) what it means to you to be on this journey with them. Remember, God wants us to love and encourage one another.

Keystone Scriptures
for Restoring My Heart

NOW MEMORIZE THESE KEYSTONE SCRIPTURES:

When I feel hurt or brokenhearted God binds up my wounds and cures my pain and sorrow.

Psalm 147:3 (AMP)

If my heart is broken, I'll find God right there; if I'm kicked in the gut, He'll help me catch my breath.

Psalm 34:18 (The Message)

Make a clean heart in me, O God. Give me a new spirit that will not be moved.

Psalm 51:10 (NLV)

LET US PRAY.

Heavenly Father,

We are so grateful You wish to restore our hearts by bringing us on this restorative journey. We long to be whole, healed, and filled with Your joy, for the joy of the Lord is our strength. As we begin exploring broken rooms of our hearts, may we feel Your agape love and presence.

In Jesus' name, Amen.

Chapter

TWO

RESTORING MY MIND

"… Even those from afar shall come and build the temple of the Lord. Then you shall know that the Lord of hosts has sent Me to you …"

Zechariah 6:15 (NKJV)

SUPPLIES

For this chapter's Heartwork, you will need a pen or pencil and your *Heart Journey™ Journal.*

As you complete your Inventory Your Thinking Heartwork, let lies that have bogged you down like wet blankets slip off as you receive the truth of God's Word that will heal your soul and lighten your load. Then, we will discover another formidable reframe tool.

INDIVIDUAL HEARTWORK – INVENTORY YOUR THINKING

Complete the chart below, turning around your thinking errors into truth, one by one.

Describe a situation where you recently experienced a challenge.	How do you feel about it?	What is the automatic thought or belief about yourself?	From what category is the thought? Defectiveness, Safety, or Trust?	What is a more helpful (and/or scriptural) thought?	How do you feel when you think about it with more helpful/ positive thoughts?
e.g., My sister drove off without saying goodbye.	e.g., I feel sad and hurt.	e.g., I am not lovable.	e.g., I am defective.	e.g., She may have been triggered and angry, but I am still lovable. My friends love me. Ps 27:10 God loves me when family does not show love.	e.g., I feel less sad, comforted.

Heart **Journey**

Describe a situation where you recently had a challenge.	How do you feel?	What is the automatic thought or belief about yourself?	From what category is the thought? Defectiveness, Safety, Trust	What is a more helpful (and/or scriptural) thought?	How do you feel when you think about it with more helpful/positive thoughts?
e.g., The team ignored me in the meeting.	e.g., Angry, Embarrassed.	e.g., No one is ever there for me.	e.g., I cannot trust anyone.	e.g., The team was likely just nervous because we had a new team leader. I can trust Shay. She never gossips and is kind.	e.g., I feel less angry, happier, more content.

MIND MANSION™ ACTIVITY

Now that you have learned about Mind Mansion™ as a power tool (from reading Heart Journey), it is your turn to experience how it works. In what rooms do you want to spend time within your Mind Mansion™? How do you want to interact with Jesus in your Mind Mansion™? What rooms do you and He want to redecorate?

As you work on your Mind Mansion™ Heartwork, use your holy imagination to bring forth the fruit of love, joy, and peace into your mind. Choose rooms that will regulate you and welcome Jesus into every room with you.

MIND MANSION™ ACTIVITY

Sit or lie down in a comfortable place and imagine your mind as an expansive mansion with millions of rooms. Some of these rooms are familiar, but we are going into some new and refreshing rooms. What room do you want to go into? Remember, in your Mind Mansion™, there are no limits to the goodness you can experience. Look around and enjoy all the pleasant rooms that you can visit.

Then imagine that you hear a gentle knock echoing through the corridors of your Mind Mansion™. Your heart leaps with joy as you open the door, revealing Jesus standing before you, His face adorned with a delighted expression.

Jesus has come to spend the entire day with you, pouring out His love and cherishing your presence. Feel His embrace of unconditional acceptance and compassion enveloping you. Allow His love to fill every fiber of your being, dissolving any doubts or insecurities that may linger within your heart. His presence fills every room of your Mind Mansion™.

As you stand beside Jesus, envision the limitless possibilities that lie before you. Ask yourself, "What would I like to do with Jesus? Where do I want to go in my Mind Mansion™?" Imagine yourselves embarking on a grand adventure together, exploring the depths of your shared connection and experiencing the beauty of His Presence. Whether it's strolling through fields of wildflowers, sitting by a tranquil lake, or engaging in heartfelt conversations, the choice is yours.

As the day unfolds, feel the tender touch of Jesus as He meets every need of your heart. Allow His love to wash away any pain or burden you may carry, replacing it with a profound sense of peace and restoration. Take a moment to envision the two of you redecorating rooms within your Mind Mansion™. Watch as the rooms transform, reflecting the beauty, truth, and love that Jesus brings into your life. As you collaborate with Jesus in this act of redecoration, feel the power of His presence infusing every corner of your mind with His divine grace and transformative love.

Take a deep breath and savor the joyous moments you shared with Jesus. Breathe in His presence as you open your eyes.

Now write down what you experienced.

Use this QR code to access audible versions of activities.

INDIVIDUAL HEARTWORK – PLEASANT THOUGHTS (IN YOUR MIND MANSION™)

Now write down a list of pleasant thoughts from your Mind Mansion(TM), or that you enjoy pondering. You can come back to this list anytime you need a mood boost and think about these delightful thoughts.

ENRICH WITH POSITIVE MEMORIES ACTIVITY

Get into a comfortable spot in a chair or on a bed or couch, and begin to drift back in time in your mind thinking about the feeling of security and belonging, and when you felt those feelings most in your life. Let your mind roll over your memories, finding experiences or seasons in your life where this sense of belonging was keenly strong. Imagine that sense of belonging is a color or a texture in your body. What color or texture would it be? Let us say you identified the color as pink. Ask Jesus, "Help me find more pink times of belonging in my history." With Jesus, roll through your past collecting these times like treasures. Your goal is to find memories that are uncorrupted by negativity.

Use this QR code to access audible versions of activities.

For many women, this exercise can be difficult because the trauma vortex inside of you is drawing all your attention away from positive memories. We will use the uncoupling tool for this. The uncoupling skill is illustrated below.

UNCOUPLING ACTIVITY

Ask Jesus, "Lord, help me uncouple this memory from pain so I can enjoy belonging and goodness." Identify a positive memory that has some corruption (negative feeling) clouding your enjoyment of the memory. Take a moment to look around the room you are currently in and choose an object that evokes a positive feeling that can be associated with a positive memory. The item can be anything—a pillow, a picture, a window—as long as it can represent a positive experience for you. Next, select an object in the room that represents the negative emotions associated with the positive memory. Again, the item can be anything—a trash can, a pile of papers—as long as it can represent the negative feeling. Now continue to meditate on the positive memory being separated from the negative feelings. Validate within yourself your negative feelings, "Yes I feel this pain," while at the same time allowing the object in the room that represents the negative emotions to be a holding place and container for those negative emotions. Imagine Jesus holding the object and all the negative feelings for you. Now allow yourself to more fully be with the positive memory. Now what if that positive feeling were a color? Identify the color and deepen the experience, imagining the positivity and the color lavishing through your body as Jesus rejoices with you.

Use this QR code to access audible versions of activities.

SAFE PLACE ACTIVITY

Remember, your safe place can be as big as you want, and it can be an inside space, an outside space, or both. There are no limits as long as we stay in the realm of what God would consider good according to His word.

To start this exercise, make sure you are in a comfortable place and that you can feel the seat under you, whether it is a chair, couch, or bed, wherever you can feel grounded and in touch with the surface supporting you.

Most people close their eyes, or if you prefer, keep them open. Let us start by welcoming Jesus into this place. Breathe in His spirit. Now, imagine a safe place that either you have been to or to which you could imagine going. It could be a special room or place just for you. And in this place, we do not want anyone else there. If angels give you a sense of security, they can be there, but no one other than Jesus.

Using your imagination, look around at this safe place. What do you see? What do you hear? Think about the sounds you hear that are so soothing to your soul. Let yourself know everything is okay, and it is right to experience this comfort even now.

What do you feel in this very safe, protective place, knowing that everything there is just for you? Maybe there are smells that delight and soothe you. What are those smells? Breathe them in, knowing everything is okay and you have everything you need. Maybe there are even things to taste in this safe place. Just enjoy everything around you, softening more and more into a sense of safety, knowing you can come to this safe place at any time.

Now we are going to use a skill called Pneumaception™. "Pneuma" "ception" means "Spirit" "ception" and refers to the ability to sense or perceive the Presence or movement of the Holy Spirit. Jesus said, "My sheep, hear My voice," and you have the ability to hear what the Spirit of God is saying to you. Jesus is right here with you in this very safe place. There is no one safer than Jesus. Ask Jesus what He would like to say to you and listen as He lavishes you with love and belonging. Ask Him to show you what safety through Him looks and feels like. Sit in His Presence and let Him wash over you with waves of safety and love.

Notice that you can come here and be safe, and your soul can be soothed within your Safe Place with Jesus any time. As you drink in more comfort and love, begin to wiggle your fingers and toes. Let yourself slowly open your eyes if they were closed, knowing everything is working for good in your life according to Romans 8:28.

Now, tuck that big expansive, safe place on the inside of you in your heart home so you can go there anytime you want. Writing about it in your journal, drawing, or painting it would be a great way to help you remember it and all its details.

Use this QR code to access audible versions of activities.

EYES OF JESUS™ ACTIVITY

As you engage in the Eyes of Jesus™ activity, allow yourself to be enveloped in His love, knowing that as His love heals your heart, you will receive more and more over time, just as Jesus said in Matthew 13:12 (TPT): "For everyone who listens with an open heart will receive progressively more revelation until he has more than enough…"

EYES OF JESUS™ ACTIVITY

Find a comfortable spot, perhaps a chair or couch, and begin to become aware that Jesus is with you, around you, and inside you. Close your eyes if that is comfortable, and soften into the presence of the Lord, who is literally the Spirit of love. Allow your thoughts to meditate on a massive blue pool filled with liquid love. Now as you zoom in more closely looking at this lavish deep blue pool of love, I wonder if you could imagine recognizing that this is the same love pouring out through the eyes of Jesus toward you. Vast and expansive pools of love are flowing from the eyes of Jesus into every space of your soul. Imagine His love decadently pouring over the inside of you, around you, above you, below you, slathering you with love, belonging, and adoration such as you have never felt before. Allow yourself to move more deeply into the pools of love within the eyes of Jesus, moving from the shallow into the deep as He loves and enjoys you with the purest love possible. Allow yourself to soften even more into this love surrounding you that is now in and through you. Now consider drinking in the water that is pure love. You are like a small sponge in a vast sea of love with glorious abundance surrounding you. Soak in more of that love, drink in more of that love. And now, as you are ready, wiggle your fingers and toes, knowing you can come back to this place anytime. If your eyes are closed, open them. Commit to yourself to go back and drink of this love through the eyes of Jesus several times a day.

Use this QR code to access audible versions of activities.

I pray you come back to drink soul nourishment from the eyes of Jesus several times a day.

Beloved, in your Heartwork, you will make a list for Enrich with Imagery assets. Invest time and deep thought in these assets daily as a source of comfort to nurture your emotional well-being. Connect heart-to-heart with Jesus in these spaces.

After you complete your Individual Heartwork for Enrich with Imagery, we will discover skills that increase your mental and emotional vigor by catching the "foxes that ruin your vineyards in bloom" (Song of Solomon 2:15).

INDIVIDUAL HEARTWORK – ENRICH WITH IMAGERY

1. Describe ways you can use your holy imagination to increase peace and love in your life.

2. List five safe memories you can use to self-calm (e.g., Deborah remembers Grandma always keeping cookies in the cookie jar because Grandma loved her).

3. List five safe images you can use to self-soothe (e.g., mountain images, beach images, an image of Jesus).

4. Describe your safe place in-depth including sights, sounds, and descriptions of the five-senses.

5. Write down all Jesus revealed to you in the Enrich with Imagery activities.

INDIVIDUAL HEARTWORK – STRUCTURE YOUR LIFE

1. Seek the guidance of Jesus to discern between assignments that originate from Him and those that do not align with His will for how you spend your time. Take a moment to pause and invite Him to reveal to you His divine assignments. Write below what He shows you.

2. List energy-drainers you can reduce in your life.

3. List life-giving activities you want to maintain or increase in your life.

4. Let us cultivate awareness of your values and how they are tied to your use of time. It is time to cultivate awareness of how you are spending your time and energy. List your top five values (e.g., put God first; show kindness; prioritize family time; enjoy the journey; and know and fulfill my purpose).

5. Create a pie chart based on how you use your time. Shade in slices of this circle to indicate how much time you use for daily life activities. Here are possible categories: work, play, social activities, hobbies, time with friends, recreation, sleep, volunteer work, spiritual disciplines, and development (e.g., study, prayer, confession, worship, fellowship, rest, celebration, service), family time, me-time, fitness, meal planning and nutrition, date time, etc.

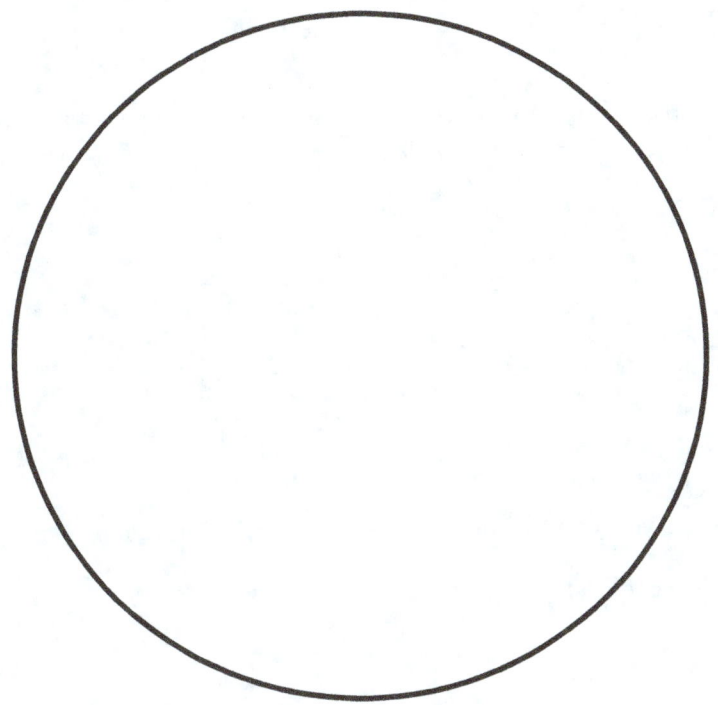

6. Now list your top five values in order of importance.

7. Compare your top five values with your time use. What do you want to change to align more with your values?

8. Ask Jesus, "What do I need to prune regarding my stewardship of time?" Write down what He says below.

9. List ways you can live more restfully in each domain.

   a. Physical Rest

   b. Mental Rest

   c. Emotional Rest

d. Social Rest (increasing safe social support)

e. Sensory Rest

f. Creative Rest

g. Spiritual Rest

10. List the names of people with whom you have life-giving relationships, and with whom you want to foster closer relationships at this time.

11. List the names of people with whom you feel drained and with whom you can decrease time.

12. What is your plan for graciously decreasing time with those for whom you are low on grace?

13. List your commitments to edit your life below and then speak each statement out loud. Let a friend know of your plans for accountability.

I will increase time doing _____ by _____% a (circle: day, week, or month).

I will increase time doing _____ by _____% a (circle: day, week, or month).

I will increase time doing _____ by _____% a (circle: day, week, or month).

I will decrease time doing _____ by _____% a (circle: day, week, or month).

I will decrease time doing _____ by _____% a (circle: day, week, or month).

INDIVIDUAL HEARTWORK – STAYING IN MY WINDOW

Now, take time to reflect and journal your responses to the following questions:

1. What triggers bump you out for the Window of Tolerance?

2. What strategies did you come into this study with that help you enter back into the Window of Tolerance once your nervous system is hyper-aroused?

3. What strategies did you come into this study with that help you enter back into the Window of Tolerance once your nervous system is hypo-aroused?

4. Which techniques and exercises have we reviewed so far that you feel will benefit you? Why?

5. What themes and lies from the enemy did you discover in the reframing exercises?

6. How has the Mind Mansion™ tool been effective for you?

7. What imagery has been impactful in stabilizing your life?

8. What changes are you committed to making regarding restructuring your life?

HEART GROUP DISCUSSION - TIME TO SHARE.

Remember, a lot of healing can occur when you share with a trusted friend or family member, or your small group. If you feel comfortable doing so, take time now to share your thoughts on the following:

1. Are you excited about your Heart Journey™ toward restoration and wholeness, or does the thought of giving up old habits make you uncomfortable? Why?

2. As we review areas of our heart home that may need restoration, especially energy-drainers and energy-givers, think of at least one simple change you can make toward increasing the energy-givers vs. the energy-drainers. Share in the space below.

3. When we prepare to delve into heart home improvements, we have to learn to utilize new tools, making it imperative to pray for one another. In the space below, make a note of different ways you can pray for your sisters in Christ.

4. What Scripture has Jesus placed on your heart this week that will promote your healing through restored emotions?

5. How has Jesus used this Scripture to encourage you? As we walk this journey, Jesus uses our encouraging stories to lift up others.

Keystone Scriptures
for Restoring My Mind

NOW MEMORIZE THESE KEYSTONE SCRIPTURES:

As he thinks in his heart, so is he.

Proverbs 23:7 (NLV)

God has not given me a spirit of fear, but of power, love, and a sound mind.

2 Timothy 1:7 (KJV)

I strip myself of my former nature (put off and discard my old unrenewed self) which characterized my previous manner of life. I am constantly being renewed in the spirit of my mind (having a fresh mental and spiritual attitude), and I put on the new nature (the regenerate self) created in God's image, (Godlike) in true righteousness and holiness.

Ephesians 4:22-24 (AMP)

LET US PRAY.

Heavenly Father,

Again, we are so grateful that You have brought us on this healing journey, especially with sisters in Christ who can help bear our burdens. We pray You will be with each one studying this lesson as she works toward renovating the innermost chambers of her heart.

In Jesus' name, Amen.

Chapter

THREE

RESTORING MY NERVOUS SYSTEM

Do you not know that your body is a temple of the Holy Spirit within you, whom you have from God? You are not your own, for you were bought with a price.

So glorify God in your body.

1 Corinthians 6:19-20 (ESV)

SUPPLIES

For this chapter's Heartwork, you will need a pen or pencil, colored pencils or markers, and your *Heart Journey*™ *Journal.*

Reconciling with our bodies and paying attention to our inner life enables us to integrate fully with our bodies and with the Lord. Grounding is a vital aspect of our healing journey, and it is normal to struggle with allowing body sensations to move through and out of our bodies. However, by finding an anchor or a place of stability in our bodies, we can become fully present and available to the Lord.

This integration allows us to be used by Him in every aspect of our being, which is a beautiful and powerful experience. Together, we will scan our bodies with curiosity and attention, identifying positive sensations and using them to find stability and peace. This exercise can be a powerful tool in helping you regulate your emotions and feel more present in your body.

OCCUPY THE BODY: GROUNDING ACTIVITY

Find a cozy seat or lay down on a bed or couch. Take a moment to turn your attention inward and focus on your body's sensations. Close your eyes if you like. Slowly scan from your head down to your toes, noticing what you feel along the way. As you scan, look for sensations in your body that are positive. Are you aware of the support of the chair or bed beneath you? Feel the support your body experiences as it reposes.

Now start with the top of your head. Scan throughout your head and neck. What sensations are you feeling? Is there anywhere in your head and neck that feel particularly good? If so, where are you feeling that sensation? What sensation are you feeling? Next, we will drop down to your chest, back, and arms. Holding an attitude of curiosity, what are you experiencing now? Can you name any positive sensations? Remember that Jesus is with you in the experience and so am I. Slowly drop down into your tummy and your bottom areas, and into your thighs, legs, and feet. What positive sensations can you find?

Now, let us ground by identifying the most positive sensation you found, and stay there for a bit. Where did you experience the most anchoring in your body? Let us go to that place and remain curious about what will happen next. Follow that positive sensation in your body. If it were a color or texture, what might it be? Perhaps it is pink and warm. If so, focus on that pink warmness and see if you can soften into it a bit more, a teaspoon more. Soften into the good, as an anchor. Soften into the security of feeling some comfort and peace in your body. Linger with your attention where you have positive sensations. Notice that the Holy Spirit is there with you in body and is as close as your breath.

Now wiggle your fingers and toes, and gently open your eyes knowing that you can come back to this grounded place any time you like.

Use this QR code to access audible versions of activities.

OCCUPY THE BODY: BODY SOOTHING ACTIVITY

Body soothing is very similar to grounding; the only difference is the starting place. With body resourcing we help ourselves into the process by starting out with a positive stimulus and then move into the body. You can use this tool one of two ways:

1. *Body Soothing with five senses: Find something that is pleasant for one or more of your five senses (e.g., light a pleasant smelling candle). As you enjoy the pleasurable stimulus, what do you feel in your body? What pleasant sensations do you feel? Where are those sensations? If those sensations are a color or texture, what would they be?*

2. *Body Soothing with positive memory: Find a positive memory that elicits positive body sensations. As you think about the positive memory, what do you feel in your body? What pleasant sensations do you feel? Where are those sensations? If those sensations were a color or texture, what would they be?*

Continue to attend to and expand the positive sensations, just as we did with grounding.

Use this QR code to access audible versions of activities.

OCCUPY THE BODY: TRACKING ACTIVITY

Through the power and love of God, we can listen with loving attention to the areas of our bodies that are over-activated or under-activated during times of emotional duress. By practicing tracking, we can identify the distressful feelings that cause the imbalance and release them. As you practice tracking, remember to remain curious and try to not narrate a story of why you feel what you feel. Just be with the sensations as you are also with Jesus. If at any time it feels like too much, stop and turn your attention to your grounding/anchoring sensations or go do something fun. Let us begin.

Find a cozy seat or lay down on a bed or couch. Take a moment to turn your attention inward and focus on your body sensations. We will be looking for bodily sensations of duress or emotional negativity that is held within your body. In addition, orient to the presence of God that is within you and around you, take a deep breath in and out, experiencing His spirit flowing in and out of you. Meditate on Jesus who is within you and the safety you have within Him.

Slowly scan from your head down to your toes, noticing what you feel along the way. As you scan, look for sensations in your body that are negative. Remain in fellowship with the Lord, tracking both what is happening in your body and being aware of His presence always with you. Are you aware of the support of the chair or bed beneath you? Feel the support your body experiences as it reposes.

Now, start with the top of your head. Scan throughout your body. What sensations are you feeling? Where is there a negative sensation? Where are you feeling that sensation? What sensation are you feeling? Allow yourself to be curious about the sensation, not fearful, but curious. Tune in to the loving Spirit of God within you and His love for every part of your body, allow perfect love to cast out fear as you remain curious about your body's sensations.

Try to stay with the negative sensation, asking yourself, what is happening now. Know that Jesus is with you, and you are not alone. Is the sensation moving or staying still? Is it changing? How so? If it were a color or texture, what would it be? How is it moving now? Notice how manageable the sensation is when you allow yourself to be curious about it. Continue to attend to Jesus and the bodily distress with curiosity for five more minutes if you can do so.

Use this QR code to access audible versions of activities.

INDIVIDUAL HEARTWORK – OCCUPY THE BODY

Now it is time for you to practice your Occupy the Body skills.

1. Here are a few definitions:

    a. **Grounding**: Find a settled, anchored, grounded area in the body and turn your attention to that place, with curiosity. Allow your awareness

to perceive the presence of the Lord, full of His love, mercy, and compassion within you.

b. **Body Soothing**: Engage with real or imagined positive stimuli (e.g., a rose, warm water, scent of cinnamon) using one or more of the five senses, and use curiosity and attention to follow positive sensations in the body. Allow your awareness to perceive the presence of the Lord, full of His love, mercy, and compassion within you.

c. **Tracking**: Listen with curious attention to the area of the body that is over-activated or under-activated during duress and follow the sensations with loving attention. Allow your awareness to perceive the presence of the Lord, full of His love, mercy, and compassion within you.

2. Work with Grounding:

   a. What time(s) each day will you practice Grounding?

   b. Write about your experience with Grounding.

3. Work with Body Soothing:

   a. What time(s) each day will you practice Body Soothing?

b. List ten stimuli that will help you enter into Body Soothing (e.g., essential oil).

c. Write about your experience with Body Soothing.

4. Work with Tracking:

a. What time(s) each day will you practice Tracking?

b. List four situations that cause you mild distress in which you can practice Tracking.

c. Write about your experience with Tracking.

Daily Homework—occupy your body by spending time Grounding and Tracking, always remembering that the Lord is with you in your body.

INDIVIDUAL HEARTWORK – UNDERGIRD WITH SUPPORT

1. Take an inventory of yourself in regard to how safe you are in your relationships. Rate yourself 1-10 on each item below:

Relationally Safe Characteristics	Rating 1-10
Honesty: Safe people are truthful and honest with themselves and others.	
Empathy: Safe people are empathetic and can put themselves in other people's shoes. They are sensitive to others' feelings and experiences.	
Dependability: Safe people are reliable and dependable. They keep their promises and follow through on commitments.	
Boundaries: Safe people know and respect their own boundaries, as well as others' boundaries. They do not overstep or manipulate.	
Accountability: Safe people take responsibility for their actions and behaviors. They own their mistakes and apologize when necessary.	
Non-judgmental: Safe people are non-judgmental and accepting. They do not shame or criticize others for their thoughts, feelings, or actions.	
Supportive: Safe people are supportive and encouraging. They provide emotional support and are willing to help.	
Confidentiality: Safe people keep confidences and do not gossip or share personal information without permission.	

Respectful: Safe people are respectful and considerate of others' feelings and opinions. They do not dismiss or invalidate others.	
Kindness: Safe people are kind and compassionate toward others, showing empathy and understanding.	
Consistency: Safe people are consistent in their behaviors and actions, providing a sense of stability and predictability.	
Self-awareness: Safe people are self-aware, recognizing their own strengths and weaknesses and how they impact others.	
Good communication skills: Safe people have good communication skills, allowing for clear and effective communication.	
Forgiving: Safe people are forgiving and do not hold grudges. They are willing to work through conflicts and move forward.	

2. Now sit before the Lord and ask Him how He wants to work in you to become a safer person. Rest assured, we all need to grow here. Write down what the Lord says and ask Him to work within you in this area. Commit to grow with His help in the area(s) He identifies.

3. Now, we will work on mapping out our relationships. Map out your social support, placing everyone who is meaningful in your life on the Social-gram™ below. Place those you feel closest to in the inner circle and those you feel more distant from around the edges. Include everyone meaningful or with whom you have moderate social interaction within your life including family, church, small group, friends, coworkers, neighbors, etc.

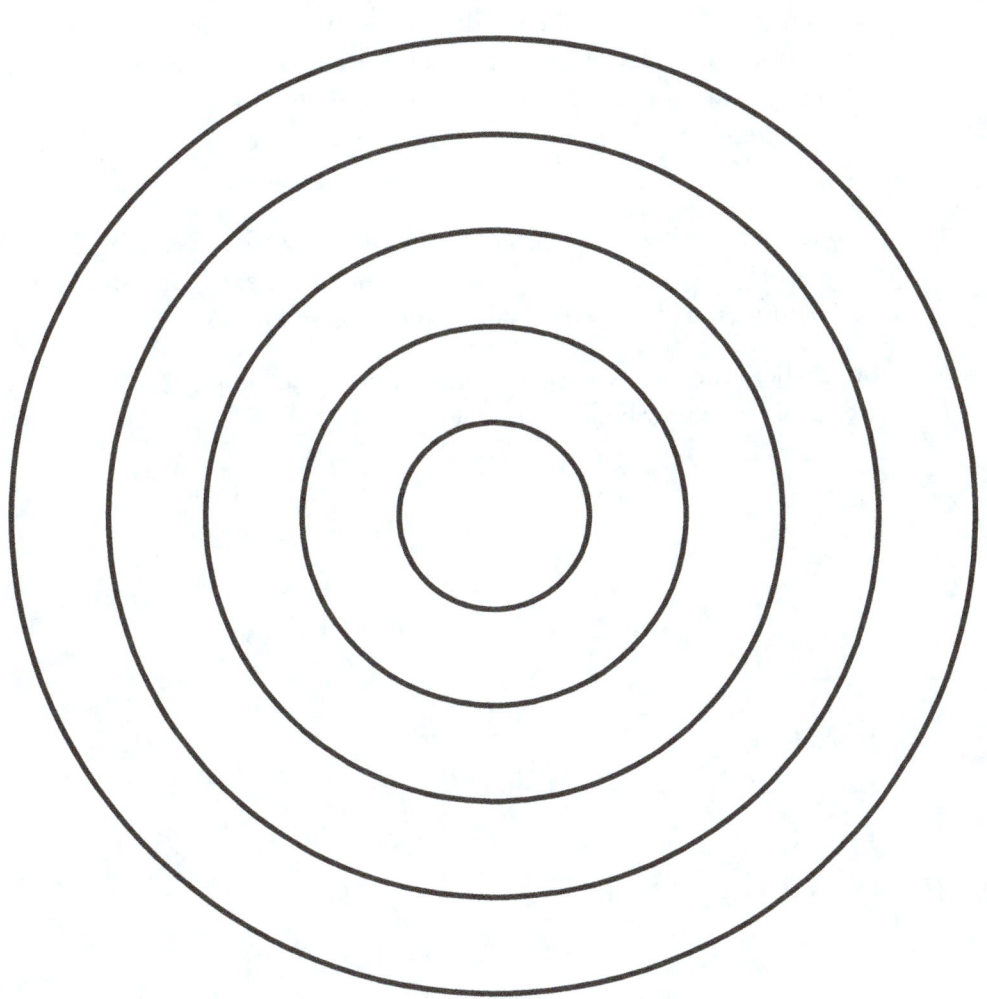

ADDITIONAL TIPS FOR YOUR SOCIALGRAM™ WORK:

- Put the people you are closest to in the center … the people you share all the different parts of your life with and/or the people with whom you spend the most time.

- If you have people where there are some cut-off relationships or a one-way cutoff, you can put them in the corners outside of the Socialgram™, if you want to acknowledge them. Sometimes people cut us out of their lives, but we did not want them cut out. Conversely, occasionally we have needed to set a boundary, and even if we have forgiven, we cannot be with certain people because they may be toxic or dangerous. These people can go in the corners outside of the Socialgram™.

4. Get out your markers or colored pencils. Circle safe, unsafe, and unsure people using different colors. Circle those who are safe with green, those who are moderately safe with yellow, and those who are unsafe with red.

5. Notice where the unsafe people are versus the safe people. Do you see any patterns? If so, describe them below:

6. Now take a purple marker and circle those people you believe to be available.

7. List the safe and available people that you will choose to spend more time with as you go through this journey.

8. With whom will you be checking in weekly?

9. What shifts will you make in your relationships to relate more often to safe people?

CHRISTIAN PROGRESSIVE RELAXATION ACTIVITY

Progressive muscle relaxation is a technique that reverses the body's physiological response to stress by intentionally tensing and releasing specific muscle groups. It is essential to listen to your body during this exercise and stop immediately if you experience any pain or discomfort. Allow the Holy Spirit to guide you through this process of relaxation and healing.

As you begin this exercise, invite the Lord to be present with you as you seek physiological relaxation. He abides within you and His breath, His Ruach, fills you.

Practice His presence throughout this activity. You will go through a process of taking a deep breath in and tensing certain muscle groups in a specific area of your body. You will hold the tension for a moment, really feeling the muscles tightening. Then, you will release the tension and allow the muscles to relax completely. Then you will breathe in and out deeply, breathing in the Ruach of God, and breathing out stress.

Disclaimer: Before starting this activity, please make sure you are in a safe and comfortable position. If at any point during the meditation you experience pain, discomfort, or any other unpleasant sensations, feel free to stop or adjust the practice as necessary. Only participate in activities that your primary care physician would recommend for you.

CHRISTIAN PROGRESSIVE RELAXATION ACTIVITY

Begin by taking a deep breath in, imagining the breath of God filling you. Then, as you exhale, let go of any tension in your body. Take another deep breath, and as you exhale, allow your body to relax even more. Notice that God is there to fill you.

Now, bring your awareness to your feet. Take a moment to feel your feet touching the ground, and imagine the Holy Spirit filling them with peace and light. As you inhale, tense the muscles in your feet, and hold the muscle tension and your breath for about five to ten seconds. Then, as you exhale, release the tension and feel all your muscles becoming more relaxed. Take a deep breath in, breathing in the breath of God, and exhaling the stress. Repeat the deep breath and exhale five more times without any muscle tension.

Move your attention up to your legs. Feel the weight of your legs sinking into the ground, and imagine the Holy Spirit bringing healing and comfort to them. As you inhale, tense the muscles in your calves and thighs, and hold the muscle tension and your breath for about five to ten seconds. Then, as you exhale, release the tension and feel all your muscles becoming more relaxed. Take a deep breath in, breathing in the breath of God, and exhaling the stress. Repeat the deep breath and exhale five more times without any muscle tension.

Next, bring your awareness to your bottom and hips. Imagine the Holy Spirit filling your bottom and hips with warmth and love, and as you inhale, tense the muscles in this area, and hold the muscle tension and your breath for about five to ten seconds. Then, as you exhale, release the tension and feel all your muscles becoming more relaxed. Take a deep breath in, breathing in the breath of God, and exhaling the stress. Repeat the deep breath and exhale five more times without any muscle tension.

Move up to your stomach and chest. Take a deep breath and feel your belly expanding, then exhale and feel your chest relaxing. Imagine the Holy Spirit bringing peace and healing to your stomach and chest. As you inhale, tense the muscles in your stomach and chest, and hold the muscle tension and your breath for about five to ten seconds. Then, as you exhale, release the tension and feel all your muscles becoming more relaxed. Take a deep breath in, breathing in the breath of God, and exhaling the stress. Repeat the deep breath and exhale five more times without any muscle tension.

Bring your attention to your arms and hands. Feel your arms resting comfortably at your sides, and imagine the Holy Spirit filling your arms and hands with love and light. As you inhale, tense the muscles in your arms and hands, and hold the muscle tension and your breath for about five to ten seconds. Then, as you exhale, release the tension and feel all your muscles becoming more relaxed. Take a deep breath in, breathing in the breath of God, and exhaling the stress. Repeat the deep breath and exhale five more times without any muscle tension.

Finally, bring your awareness to your head and neck. Imagine the Holy Spirit filling your head and neck with peace and clarity. As you inhale, tense the muscles in your neck and face, and hold the muscle tension and your breath for about five to ten seconds. Then, as you exhale, release the tension and feel all your muscles becoming more relaxed. Take a deep breath in, breathing in the breath of God, and exhaling the stress. Repeat the deep breath and exhale five more times without any muscle tension.

Take a moment to feel your whole body relaxed and at ease, filled with the light and love of the Holy Spirit. You may choose to stay in this relaxed state for a few more breaths, or slowly begin to bring your awareness back to the present moment.

Repeat as many times as you like.

Use this QR code to access audible versions of activities.

CHRISTIAN DIAPHRAGMATIC BREATHING ACTIVITY

With practice, Christian Diaphragmatic Breathing can become an effective way to manage stress and promote relaxation.

Begin by sitting comfortably in a chair or lying down on your back with your knees bent. Place one hand on your chest and the other hand on your belly. Now, take a deep breath in through your nose, and as you do, feel your belly expand like a balloon. As you breathe in, receive the breath of God filling your being from head to toe. Keep breathing in until you feel your chest start to rise.

Fill up with that breath, and then slowly exhale through your mouth, pushing all the air out of your lungs until your belly naturally pulls back in. As you exhale, you may want to purse your lips together, as if you were blowing out a candle.

Now try it again. Breathe in through your nose, feel your belly expand, and hold for a moment. Fill up with the breath of God. Exhale slowly through your mouth, letting your belly naturally pull back in. Keep breathing like this for a few more breaths, in through your nose and out through your mouth.

As you continue to breathe, try to focus on the breath of God filling you and let any earthly thoughts or distractions fade. Focus on being filled by Him and fellowshipping with His Spirit. Repeat as many times as you like.

Use this QR code to access audible versions of activities.

Remember, if at any time you feel discomfort or pain, please stop the exercise and consult a healthcare professional.

CHRISTIAN FOUR SQUARE BREATHING ACTIVITY

Another effective technique for managing anxiety is called "four square breathing." It involves taking a deep breath in through your nose for four counts, then holding that breath for four counts. Next, slowly exhale for four counts, and then hold your breath out for another four counts. While doing this, you can visualize drawing a square in your mind or on paper to help focus your attention.

We will again be meditating on and receiving the breath of God through this exercise. Let us try this breathing technique together now:

Inhale for four seconds. As you inhale, imagine that you are breathing in the breath of God, the essence of life.

Hold your breath for four seconds.

Exhale for four seconds. As you exhale, imagine that you are releasing all of your stress and anxiety.

Hold four seconds before breathing in again.

Repeat seven to ten times or for as long as you need to feel calm and centered.

Use this QR code to access audible versions of activities.

CHRISTIAN BODY SCAN ACTIVITY

In this activity, tune into your body and invite the Holy Spirit to guide you. Start by finding a comfortable seated position with your feet planted firmly on the ground.

Close your eyes and take a deep breath in, imagining the Holy Spirit filling your lungs with air. As you exhale, release any tension or stress in your body. Take a few more deep breaths like this, allowing your body to relax with each exhale.

Now, focus your attention on the top of your head. Imagine the Holy Spirit gently guiding your awareness through your body, from the crown of your head, down to your forehead, and then to your eyes. Let go of any tension you may be holding in these areas and invite the Holy Spirit to bring peace and calm.

Next, bring your attention down to your jaw, neck, and shoulders. Let go of any tightness or constriction you may be holding in these areas, inviting the Holy Spirit to release any tension and bring relaxation.

Continue scanning your body, moving down to your chest, back, and stomach. Invite the Holy Spirit to fill these areas with peace and love, allowing any stress or tension to melt away.

Next, bring your attention to your arms, hands, and fingers. Imagine the Holy Spirit bringing warmth and relaxation to these areas, releasing any tightness or discomfort you may be feeling.

Finally, bring your attention down to your legs, feet, and toes. Allow the Holy Spirit to fill these areas with a sense of grounding and stability, letting go of any tension or stress you may be holding.

Take a few deep breaths to conclude the meditation, feeling grateful for the presence of the Holy Spirit within you and the peace and relaxation it brings to your body.

Use this QR code to access audible versions of activities.

5, 4, 3, 2, 1 MEDITATION – CHRISTIAN VERSION ACTIVITY

Our senses are always in the present moment, and when we feel anxious, it is because our mind is focused on the future or the past. This activity will help us focus on the here and now and also on the Lord. We will take a moment to do a quick body scan and check in with ourselves before we begin.

Take a deep breath and think about how constricted your body feels, what you are feeling, and what you are experiencing. Now, start the meditation called "Five, Four, Three, Two, One - Christian Version."

Five. Begin by looking around and finding five things you can see. As you do, try to focus on the pleasurable things in your environment rather than the unpleasant ones. Name those things in your head as you see them. Thank Jesus for those five things.

Four. Next, focus on four things you can hear. Just be aware of the sounds around you in your environment. Listen to the sounds of nature, people talking or music playing. Thank Jesus for those four things.

Three. Think about three things you can feel with your skin. This could be the back of your chair supporting you or the texture of your clothing. Take a moment to recognize how your body is being supported by your surroundings. Think of it as God's love and support for you. Take a deep breath and notice the beautiful aromas in your environment. Thank Jesus for those three things.

Two. Think about two things you can smell or that you like to smell. What smells bring back good memories? Thank Jesus for those two things.

Finally, ask Jesus to name one thing He enjoys about you. Allow yourself to embrace His love and enjoyment of you.

Use this QR code to access audible versions of activities.

Remember, 5, 4, 3, 2, 1 Meditation - Christian Version can be used anytime, anywhere, especially when you are feeling anxious or stressed. It is a simple yet powerful way to center yourself in the present and in the Lord.

Beloved, please hear me on this point … I want you to practice your relaxation skills when you are not anxious! Practicing all these exercises when you are calm and peaceful can help you use them with skill and muscle-minded automaticity when anxiety sets in. Remember to check in with yourself before and after the meditation to see how it has helped you.

Now to more Heartwork! Press on, Beloved. It will all be worth it!

SELF-MOMMING™ ACTIVITY

Now that we understand the power of Self-Momming™, it is time to put it into practice with some Heartwork. Let us take a moment to connect with Jesus and ask Him to guide us as we nurture ourselves with His love and wisdom. Get ready to speak words of life to yourself and draw strength from Jesus' power and example. Let us dive into some Self-Momming™ Heartwork together.

Get into a comfortable space, and feel free to close your eyes if you like. Take a moment to identify an area where you feel insecure, unsure of yourself, or overwhelmed. At the same time, turn your attention to the Lord and notice that Jesus is right here with you. Take a deep breath in and out, and breathe in the Ruach (breath) of God. Allow yourself to soften into the emotional safety you have with the Lord. If that feeling of safety were a color or a texture, what would it be? Let the color or texture of that feeling of safety spread throughout your body. Then, think about the situation that is causing insecurity, pain, or overwhelm, and welcome Jesus into that situation using your holy imagination. Ask Jesus, "What are You saying in this situation?" Notice His kind eyes and His loving attention to you and listen to His nurturing and wise words. Let the safety and security of His grace and truth wash over you, allowing you to soften into even more of His love in this moment.

Next, get in touch with the part of you that is your most nurturing self, the part of you that is a friend, mother, or caretaker. Imagine this part of you taking hold of the hand of Jesus and being infused with His love and strength. Then, speak to the part of you that is hurt and vulnerable in this situation using HEAR (Hearing, Empathizing, Accepting, and Respecting) in a way that models after Jesus. Let the child part of you that feels the pain in this situation receive the love and acceptance that you and Jesus have to give her. Soften into even more safety, love, protection, and validation, ensuring that the needs of your most vulnerable part are being met.

And when you are ready, wiggle your fingers and toes, and open your eyes if they were closed, knowing that you can go back to this place of nurturing with the Lord and with using the Self-Momming™ tool at any time.

Use this QR code to access audible versions of activities.

PRACTICE SELF-MOMMING™

Beloved, I am so proud of you for practicing Self-Momming™. It is essential that you practice this tool daily, even several times a day, as it can also be used to bring healing to difficult memories. In future chapters, we will be using this skill to explore and heal past memories. We will welcome Jesus into those memories to bring healing and use Self-Momming™ to meet the needs of our inner child. Stay tuned for more on this use of this formidable tool in the coming chapters.

INDIVIDUAL HEARTWORK – COMFORT THROUGH SELF-MOMMING™

Journal on what you experienced during the Self-Momming™ activity.

INDIVIDUAL HEARTWORK – RELAXATION AND SELF-MOMMING™ REFLECTION

1. Practice Christian Four Square Breathing. Be sure to focus on breathing in the breath of God.

   a. Write about your experience.

   b. When will you use Christian Four Square Breathing?

2. Practice Christian Progressive Relaxation. Be sure to focus on breathing in the breath of God. *Make sure you have your physician's approval before engaging.*

    a. Write about your experience.

    b. When will you use Christian Progressive Relaxation?

3. Practice Christian Body Scan.

    a. Write about your experience.

    b. When will you use Christian Progressive Relaxation?

4.   Practice the 5, 4, 3, 2, 1 Meditation - Christian Version.

a.   Write about your experience.

b.   When will you use the 5, 4, 3, 2, 1 Meditation - Christian Version?

5.   After practicing the above Self-Momming™ activity, answer the following questions.

a.   How has Jesus interacted like a parent with you?

b.   Besides Jesus, who can you model your Self-Momming™ after?

c. Now practice Self-Momming™ by talking to your inner child as if she were your beloved daughter. Write about your experience.

d. Now think about a mildly distressing memory from your past, imagine both Jesus and your own self as mom in the memory, and allow your child to be loved through Self-Momming™ and by Jesus.

e. When will you use Self-Momming™?

INDIVIDUAL HEARTWORK – ENLIGHTEN WITH CONTENT

1. What healing content do you currently listen to?

2. List the added healing and encouraging content to which you will be exposing yourself as you are working through this Heart Journey™ (e.g., Christian programming, podcasts, audiobooks, talks, etc.).

3. List the content you will edit out of your life in order to heal your attachment system, decrease fear, and reduce distress.

INDIVIDUAL HEARTWORK – RESTORING MY NERVOUS SYSTEM

Reflect on and journal your answers to the below questions. Your journal is a great, non-judgmental listener!

1. Take a moment to reflect on your relationship with your body. Write a paragraph on your reflections regarding how you have felt about and treated your body over time.

2. How do you plan to use the grounding tools to aid in your Heart Journey™?

3. Think of at least three ways you can incorporate Jesus into your healing journey through the tools mentioned in this chapter (grounding, gaining support, and relaxation).

4. Thus far, we have covered a lot of bodily relaxation tools. Without putting extra stress on yourself, how can you recognize when a tool might be helpful to use?

5. How have you felt the presence of God with you this week while on the Heart Journey™? Reflect and journal on your interactions with Him.

6. What was the main theme that Jesus impressed on your heart as you worked through this chapter?

HEART GROUP DISCUSSION – TIME TO SHARE.

1. Take time to research Scripture you will use to support you in this phase of the journey. Share with your group or safe person why this particular Scripture resonates with you and how you plan to integrate it into your healing.

2. If you took the opportunity to integrate a grounding tool in your daily journey, share with your small group. How did it go?

3. When sharing with others, it is important not to judge, but to share, love, and encourage. Discuss ways you can help each other recognize when a tool might be helpful to use.

4. As you each have worked through the material, you were encouraged to think of different media outlets and relevant resources you could access to stay grounded in your Heartwork. Take time to share with one another your favorite podcasts, authors, videos, and other resources.

5. In today's culture, we often stay so busy, it is hard to incorporate one more thing into your daily routine. How can you incorporate the encouraging RESOURCEs into your schedule without making it a chore? Share with your small group sisters. We all could use some helpful tips!

Keystone Scriptures
for Restoring My Nervous System

NOW MEMORIZE THESE KEYSTONE SCRIPTURES:

Therefore I urge you, brothers and sisters, by the mercies of God, to present your bodies [dedicating all of yourselves, set apart] as a living sacrifice, holy and well-pleasing to God, which is your rational (logical, intelligent) act of worship.

Romans 12:1 (AMP)

Or do you not know that your body is a temple of the Holy Spirit within you, whom you have from God? You are not your own, for you were bought with a price. So glorify God in your body.

1 Corinthians 6:19-20 (ESV)

When you pass through the waters, I will be with you; and through the rivers, they shall not overwhelm you; when you walk through fire you shall not be burned, and the flame shall not consume you.

Isaiah 43:2 (ESV)

LET US PRAY.

Heavenly Father,

Thank You that we can begin healing our hearts and be renewed in Christ. Father, we love the idea of being used by You more and more every day, but we know, in order to do so, our hearts must be turned toward You, and we must be willing for You to do Your work in us. Lord, make our hearts malleable. And if there is a shambled area of our hearts where we do not see a need for renovation, Father, please guide us in Your gentle way toward complete restoration.

In Jesus' name, Amen.

Chapter

F O U R

RESTORING MY HEALTHY HABITS

But the fruit of the Spirit is love, joy, peace, patience, kindness, goodness, faithfulness, gentleness, self-control; against such things there is no law.

Galatians 5:22-23 (ESV)

SUPPLIES

For this chapter's Heartwork, you will need a pen or pencil and your *Heart Journey*™ *Journal.*

This is the stage in our journey where we focus on curbing those unhelpful behaviors, substituting them with more beneficial ones. The goal is to allow ourselves to feel emotions genuinely, without resorting to artificial means or escape or control that have consumed too much of our time and energy. Essentially, we aim to replace these behaviors with healthy coping mechanisms so we can move on to doing deeper Heartwork.

INDIVIDUAL HEARTWORK – ELIMINATE UNHELPFUL BEHAVIORS

1. List the behaviors in your life that are in excess or unhelpful. (i.e., they are hurting you as much or more than helping you).

2. Pick one unhelpful behavior above, and work through a Behavioral Chain Analysis (BCA).

    a. List the problematic behavior here. (e.g., drinking too much wine.)

    b. List setting events that make the unhelpful behavior more likely to occur. (e.g., I was home alone and felt lonely; I just had a fight with a friend.)

3. Using the chart below, start with what was occurring before the problematic behavior began. Fill in the squares from left to right, starting in the top left square. Each square will represent one event in the causal chain of events. Start with what happened just before the problematic behavior and work through to all consequences that occurred after the behavior. Include all relevant events and all your thoughts and feelings throughout the "before, during, and after" sequence.

4. Then, go back through with a different colored marker or pencil and write in what you could have done differently at each choice point. Make sure to include replacement behaviors that will meet your needs in a healthier way. Again, here is an example:

I could have used positive self talk and gone to the spa or for a walk.

I could have called a friend.

Husband called: he is working late.	I thought about my long, tiring day and about the mess in the kitchen.	I felt alone, and mad.	I felt justified in getting a bottle of wine on the way home.	I thought, I will only have a glass.
Husband called: asked if it was ok to be very late. I said OK, and did not share my feelings.	I felt alone like I did as a kid. Thought about calling my sister but did not.	I thought about throwing out the bottle but did not. I drank the whole bottle.	We fought when he got home.	I was hungover and felt very guilty and defeated for the next four days.

I could have called my sister and dumped out the bottle.

I could have forgiven myself sooner, and gotten together with a friend.

109

Now it is your turn to complete steps 3 and 4.

5. Write what you learned from this BCA that you can use the next time you are tempted to behave in an unhelpful way.

   a. Watch for times when I feel:

   b. Watch for these setting events:

   c. Watch for these thoughts:

d. Replacement behaviors I can use:

e. My accountability partner:

f. I will stay away from:

g. I can use these rewards to motivate me to do the right thing:

MY BEHAVIOR CHAIN ANALYSIS ACTIVITY

Now pick another unhelpful behavior and conduct a BCA:

1. Setting Events:

2. Using the one square for each event in the causal chain of events, list each link in the event chain from just before the problematic behavior all the way through to any consequences of the behavior. Include all relevant events and all thoughts and feelings.

3. Go back through with a different color marker and write in what you could have done different at each choice point. Make sure to include replacement behaviors that will meet your need in a healthier way.

4. Write what you learned from this BCA that you can use the next time you are tempted to behave in an unhelpful way.

a. Watch for times when I feel:

b. Watch for these setting events:

c. Watch for these thoughts:

d. Replacement behaviors I can use:

e. My accountability partner:

f. I will stay away from:

g. I can use these pleasurable activities:

h. I can use these rewards to motivate me to do the right thing:

INDIVIDUAL HEARTWORK - CONSECRATE TO THE LORD

LET US PRAY.

Now is a great time to take any distrust you may have to the Lord and ask Him to heal you during this process, consecrating you for His purpose.

Heavenly Father,

We give our lives wholly and fully to You as our Lord and Savior. Thank You for dying and rising for our sins and for our healing. We pray for so much healing … we pray that You would enter every heart, healing and rebuilding the sense of home, belonging, and safety, and freedom from terror and dismay. We pray that each person working through this Heart Journey™ process will have more security, safety, wholeness, and stability, so they can feel good about themselves and have more success in their life, relationships, and career/calling. Father bless each one. We give You this time and this process, asking that You would leave no stone unturned. Please heal every wound and restore everything, double, triple, and a hundred times over what the enemy has taken. And I pray that out of these wounds would come living water, that You would transform the ashes into beauty, for each person. Lord, bless these precious women. Draw them to You in every way.

In Jesus' name, Amen.

1. Write out your prayer of consecration to the Lord regarding this healing process.

2. List the areas in your heart and life where you are asking the Lord for healing and transformation.

INDIVIDUAL HEARTWORK - ORIENT TO RECONSTRUCTION TOOLS

Understanding the dialectic of acceptance and change is important to your healing process.

1. Share where you need to grow in acceptance.

2. Share where you need to press into transformation and change.

3. Reflect below on why Titration is important in the healing process.

4. Reflect below on why Working the Edges is important in trauma processing.

INDIVIDUAL HEARTWORK – HEALTHY BEHAVIORS

Reflect on and journal your answers to the below questions.

1. In this chapter, we addressed unwanted behaviors and replaced them with healthy substitutes. What are some unwanted behaviors you are most afraid of not being able to give up?

2. How can you incorporate Jesus more deeply into this part of your healing journey?

3. Can you think of a time when you let yourself down and did something you felt disappointed God? Did you tap into His grace, and if not, what kept you from receiving it?

4. As we make changes and heal bit by bit, we may not always live up to our own goals and expectations. What tools can you use to give yourself grace when your efforts fall short?

5. You are moving toward deep healing. Take time to write out a prayer to the Lord. Ask Him to help you receive His love and to love yourself more.

6. List your ten favorite Heart Journey™ Stability tools and write down when you will use them.

HEART GROUP DISCUSSION – TIME TO SHARE.

1. What have been some of the hardest unhealthy behaviors for you to give up and why?

2. What do you hope to replace these unhealthy behaviors with and how do you think the "new" will help in your healing?

3. Oftentimes, our unhealthy behaviors evolve from our body's response to coping with deeply rooted wounds. If you feel comfortable sharing, take time to talk about those deep-rooted wounds and how they may have driven some poor choices in the past.

4. Research Scripture for verses that can support you when you are tempted to fall back into unhealthy behaviors and patterns. Share them with your group or a safe person and discuss how you can integrate these verses into your journey.

5. Take time to share with your group or a safe person how you feel at this stage of your journey. Be sure to include any difficult thoughts or feelings you may have, as well as how they can continue supporting you. (Remember to go to the emergency room if there is ever an issue of safety).

Keystone Scriptures
for Restoring My Healthy Habits

NOW MEMORIZE THESE KEYSTONE SCRIPTURES:

Like a city that is broken down and without walls [leaving it unprotected]
Is a man who has no self-control over his spirit [and sets himself up for trouble].

Proverbs 25:28 (AMP)

Keep actively watching and praying that you may not come into temptation;
the spirit is willing, but the body is weak.

Mark 14:38 (AMP)

So submit to [the authority of] God. Resist the devil [stand firm against him] and he
will flee from you.

James 4:7 (AMP)

LET US PRAY.

Heavenly Father,

Thank You for being with us on this journey. Delving into matters of the heart can get messy, but we know Your son, Jesus, is a master at transforming our messes into beautiful messages. Father, may we continue to focus on You during this process, staying ever so close to You. Lord, if our hearts and minds wander and we get off course, please gently set us back on the path to healing as only You can do.

In Jesus' name, Amen.

Chapter

FIVE

RESTORING MY NARRATIVE

Then you will know the truth, and the truth will set you free.

John 8:32 (NIV)

SUPPLIES

For this chapter's Heartwork, you will need a pen and colored pencils for crafting your timelines. I highly recommend accessing photo albums or digital photos from your childhood and early adult life to help jog your memory in recalling significant events. If you struggle with accessing your memories, photos can be especially helpful. Additionally, I highly recommend scheduling weekly meetings with a trusted friend who can regularly check in on you and pray with you to stay connected and feel supported during this heart restoration process with Jesus. Also, a licensed psychotherapist can provide good support.

TIMELINE EXAMPLE:

Now it is time for you to make your first timeline. Below is an example of a timeline, using Deborah as our model. As you can see the positive events she can remember are listed on top of her timeline and the negative events are listed below at corresponding ages.

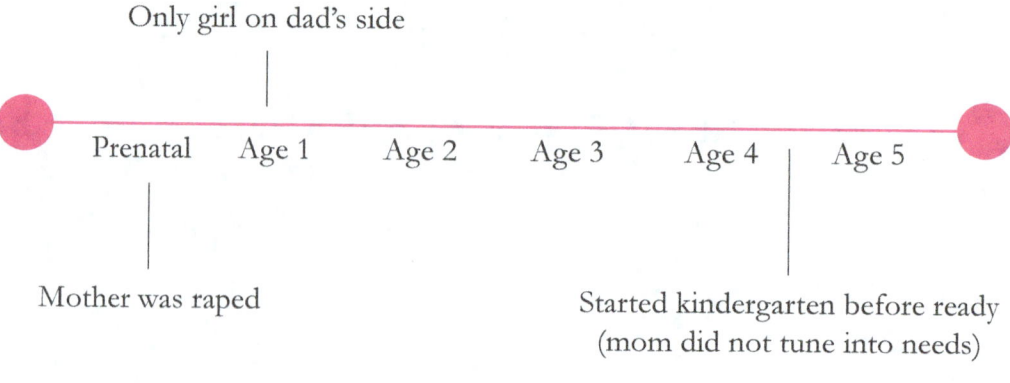

Now it is time for you to work on your timeliness through step two:

1. Write the formative positive experiences that occurred in the age range on top of the timeline, at the ages these experiences occurred.

2. Write the formative negative, wounding, traumatizing, and or painful experiences that occurred in that age range on the bottom of the timeline at the ages these experiences occurred. Remember, perception is key in trauma work, so do not judge whether or not something should be listed on the bottom of your timeline. If it feels like it should be listed, then it should be listed. Include events that happened across family and non-familial settings.

LABELING TRAUMAS AND UNMET NEEDS

After completing your timelines, get your colored pencils out for our next step. Pick a color and label every "Trauma" with a "T" with that color. Pick another color and label every "Unmet Need," with "UN." We will use this work in our next few chapters. We will work with unmet needs in the next chapter, and in Chapter

Seven, we will work with trauma. Jesus will meet you in these places! I cannot wait for you to experience His restoration!

THEMES

Now, it is time to examine your timelines and search for common themes throughout your content. Step back from the details and focus on the big picture. Negative themes that often become ingrained in our identity can usually be categorized under one of these headings: defectiveness, responsibility, safety, power and control, and trust. In your early childhood, pay attention to themes related to whether you felt safe and could trust others. Also, assess whether you felt empowered to move forward or experienced a sense of powerlessness. Identifying these themes can help us gain insight into how past experiences may have shaped our beliefs and behavior patterns.

Additionally, it is important to examine our emotional needs, such as our need for a sense of belonging and whether we have a secure foundation from which we can venture out into the world. Having parents who are a secure base means that when we are in distress, they will be there for us. While some parents may be great parents, they may not always be consistent, and it is essential to remember that safe people are consistent. We all require connection and validation of our identities to thrive.

Moreover, it is important to identify positive themes where our needs for safety, security, and physiological needs for food were met. It can be difficult to recognize the positive aspects when we are overwhelmed with negative experiences that demand our attention and validation. However, acknowledging the positive experiences can help us build resilience and find strength during challenging times.

Now it is time to explore the themes that emerge from your timelines. Take your time and reflect deeply, rather than rushing through this step. Some sample themes to consider include:

i. acceptance vs. defectiveness (e.g., I am accepted; I am bad)

ii. safety vs. unsafe (e.g., I am safe; I am not safe)

iii. trust vs. difficulty with trust (e.g., I can trust: I cannot trust anyone)

iv. power vs. feeling no power/ no control (e.g., I have power in situations: I am powerless)

   v.   belonging vs. not belonging (e.g., I belong; I do not belong)

  vi. feeling connected vs. not feeling connected (e.g., I am connected and loved
       I am alone)

INDIVIDUAL HEARTWORK – NARRATE YOUR STORY™ ACTIVITY

Identify your support people with whom you can share this journey.

Now we will work on your timelines. See below questions one to three for the timelines you will be crafting.

1.   Work on your timelines. For each timeline, mark known positive events and positive factors on the top, and negative, adverse, hurtful, and/or traumatic events on the bottom of each timeline.

2.   Label Traumas with "T" and Unmet Needs with "UN."

3.   Now work through steps one and two above on each of your timelines.

a.   Work on your zero- to five-year-old timeline.

Prenatal   Age 1   Age 2   Age 3   Age 4   Age 5

b.   Work on your elementary school years' timeline.

c.   Work on your middle school years' timeline.

d.   Work on your high school years' timeline.

e. Work on your young adult years' timeline.

f. Work on your twenties' timeline.

g. Work on your thirties' timeline (if applicable).

h. Work on your forties' to current time timeline (if applicable).

4. List themes you found while looking over your timelines—list both positive and negative themes.

   a. List positive themes you discovered as you worked through your timelines (e.g., I belong at church; I am accepted at dance).

      i. acceptance vs. defectiveness (e.g., I am accepted; I am bad)

      ii. safety vs. unsafe (e.g., I am safe; I am not safe)

      iii. trust vs. difficulty with trust (e.g., I can trust: I cannot trust anyone)

      iv. power vs. feeling no power/ no control (e.g., I have power in situations: I am powerless)

      v. belonging vs. not belonging (e.g., I belong; I do not belong)

      vi. feeling connected vs. not feeling connected (e.g., I am connected and loved I am alone)

b. List negative themes you discovered as you worked through your timelines (e.g., I am defective; something is wrong with me; I am unacceptable to peers; I have no control at night with my mom; I am not safe at home; I do not belong at school).

    i.   acceptance vs. defectiveness (e.g., I am accepted; I am bad)

    ii. safety vs. unsafe (e.g., I am safe; I am not safe)

    iii. trust vs. difficulty with trust (e.g., I can trust: I cannot trust anyone)

    iv. power vs. feeling no power/ no control (e.g., I have power in situations: I am powerless)

    v. belonging vs. not belonging (e.g., I belong; I do not belong)

    vi. feeling connected vs. not feeling connected (e.g., I am connected and loved; I am alone)

Now look over your timelines and answer these questions:

1. Make a list of all your Unmet Needs across your life that you discovered through completing the timeline work above.

2. Make a list of all your Traumas across your life that you have discovered through your timeline work.

3. Fill out a Pie of Responsibility for an event where you shared a small amount of responsibility, but the majority of the culpability was on a perpetrator of some sort.

4. Return to your unmet needs and traumas above and write one to two Scriptures that counter the lies the enemy told you that resulted in your negative themes. Meditate on these Scriptures daily.

Here are some possible Scriptures to use, or you can find your own.

- Romans 6:1-4 (ESV) - What shall we say then? Are we to continue in sin that grace may abound? By no means! How can we who died to sin still live in it? Do you not know that all of us who have been baptized into Christ Jesus were baptized into His death? We were buried therefore with Him by baptism into death, in order that, just as Christ was raised from the dead by the glory of the Father, we too might walk in newness of life.

- John 15:5 (ESV) - I am the vine; you are the branches. Whoever abides in Me and I in Him, he it is that bears much fruit, for apart from Me you can do nothing.

- 1 John 2:28 (ESV) - And now, little children, abide in Him, so that when He appears we may have confidence and not shrink from Him in shame at His coming.

- 2 Timothy 2:15 (ESV) - Do your best to present yourself to God as one approved, a worker who has no need to be ashamed, rightly handling the word of truth.

- Ephesians 5:1 (ESV) - Therefore be imitators of God, as beloved children.

- Ephesians 1:4 (ESV) - Even as he chose us in Him before the foundation of the world, that we should be holy and blameless before Him. In love.

- 2 Corinthians 3:5 (ESV) - Not that we are sufficient in ourselves to claim anything as coming from us, but our sufficiency is from God.

- Romans 8:37 (ESV) - No, in all these things we are more than conquerors through Him who loved us.

- John 15:16 (ESV) - You did not choose me, but I chose you and appointed you that you should go and bear fruit and that your fruit should abide, so that whatever you ask the Father in My name, He may give it to you.

- Colossians 1:27 (ESV) - To them God chose to make known how great among the Gentiles are the riches of the glory of this mystery, which is Christ in you, the hope of glory.

- Colossians 1:13-14 (ESV) - He has delivered us from the domain of darkness and transferred us to the kingdom of His beloved Son, in whom we have redemption, the forgiveness of sins.

- Ephesians 2:5-6 (ESV) - Even when we were dead in our trespasses, made us alive together with Christ—by grace you have been saved— and raised us up with Him and seated us with Him in the heavenly places in Christ Jesus.

- 1 Corinthians 12:12-13 (ESV) - For just as the body is one and has many members, and all the members of the body, though many, are one body,

so it is with Christ. For in one Spirit we were all baptized into one body—Jews or Greeks, slaves or free—and all were made to drink of one Spirit.

- Romans 8:39 (ESV) - Nor height nor depth, nor anything else in all creation, will be able to separate us from the love of God in Christ Jesus our Lord.

- Romans 8:29 (ESV) - For those whom He foreknew He also predestined to be conformed to the image of His Son, in order that He might be the firstborn among many brothers.

- Romans 8:14-15 (ESV) - For all who are led by the Spirit of God are sons of God. For you did not receive the spirit of slavery to fall back into fear, but you have received the Spirit of adoption as sons, by whom we cry, "Abba! Father!"

- John 15:15 (ESV) - No longer do I call you servants, for the servant does not know what his master is doing; but I have called you friends, for all that I have heard from my Father I have made known to you.

- John 3:16 (ESV) - For God so loved the world, that He gave His only Son, that whoever believes in Him should not perish but have eternal life.

- Revelation 2:17 (ESV) - He who has an ear, let him hear what the Spirit says to the churches. To the one who conquers I will give some of the hidden manna, and I will give him a white stone, with a new name written on the stone that no one knows except the one who receives it.'

- Hebrews 12:2 (ESV) - Looking to Jesus, the founder and perfecter of our faith, who for the joy that was set before Him endured the cross, despising the shame, and is seated at the right hand of the throne of God.

- Colossians 2:10 (ESV) - And you have been filled in him, who is the head of all rule and authority.

5. Write down the lies you discovered during your timeline work that you have been believing about yourself after "I renounce this lie." Then write a statement that is true based on God's Word that counteracts the lies after "I choose to believe." Say what you renounce and choose to believe out loud. For example: "I renounce this lie: I was to blame for the rape. Now I choose to believe: I was innocent and what was done to me is wrong."

I renounce this lie:
Now I choose to believe:

I renounce this lie:
Now I choose to believe:

I renounce this lie:
Now I choose to believe:

I renounce this lie:
Now I choose to believe:

I renounce this lie:
Now I choose to believe:

I renounce this lie:
Now I choose to believe:

I renounce this lie:
Now I choose to believe:

I renounce this lie:
Now I choose to believe:

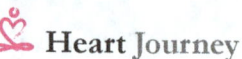

I renounce this lie:
Now I choose to believe:

I renounce this lie:
Now I choose to believe:

I renounce this lie:
Now I choose to believe:

I renounce this lie:
Now I choose to believe:

INDIVIDUAL HEARTWORK – MY JOURNEY CHECK-IN

Reflect on and journal on the questions below:

1. In this chapter, we began reviewing our pasts and the unhealthy patterns that developed. How are you feeling right now? Expound.

2. What parts of this exercise are particularly hard for you to review?

3. How can you incorporate Jesus into this part of your healing journey?

4. Research Scripture for verses that can support you when the past seems to come crashing back down. Write them below.

5. Which of these verses is your favorite for this leg of the journey and why?

HEART GROUP DISCUSSION - TIME TO SHARE.

1. What are some common themes the enemy has used to hold you back from fulfilling your God-given purpose?

2. As you review the positive events in your lifetime, what are some common themes for the happier and more joyful times?

3. Sometimes, when we get so close to overcoming a deeply rooted barrier in our lives, something comes out of nowhere and seems to knock us off course. What are some practical tools you can use to press through to victory?

4. Victory so often comes in small steps. With that being the case, what are some small steps you can take toward overcoming the enemy's influence in your life?

5. Discuss how your small group or a safe person can support you when even those small steps may seem out of reach.

Remember: Progress, not perfection!

Keystone Scriptures
for Restoring My Narrative

NOW MEMORIZE THESE KEYSTONE SCRIPTURES:

Yet in all these things we are more than conquerors and gain an overwhelming victory through Him who loved us (so much that He died for us).

Romans 8:37 (AMP)

For the Lord takes pleasure in His people;
He will beautify the humble with salvation.

Psalm 149:4 (AMP)

Then you will know the truth, and the truth will set you free.

John 8:32 (NIV)

LET US PRAY.

Heavenly Father,

We thank You so much for our pasts ... although they may not be pretty, we know You never waste a hurt. You will use it all!

Also, You specialize in turning ashes into beauty. Thank You, Father for taking our pasts and using them to make our futures bright. We love the fact that we do not have to settle for the enemy's agenda against our lives. Rather we can embrace Your agenda for our lives and allow You to rewrite the narrative.

Thank You for being with us on this journey, Father. Help us to embrace all You have in store for us with open minds and hearts.

In Jesus' name, Amen.

Chapter

SIX

RESTORING MY EMOTIONS

Come to Me, all you who are weary and burdened, and I will give you rest.

Matthew 11:28 (NIV)

SUPPLIES

As you engage with your chapter six Heartwork you will need the following materials: pen or pencil, and colored pencils or markers for drawing, and your list of "Unmet Needs" and "Themes of Unmet Needs" from your chapter five timelines.

INDIVIDUAL HEARTWORK – ORDERING UNMET NEEDS MEMORIES

Return to your Heartwork from the last chapter and find your list of unmet needs from childhood. Now, in the left column below, list your unmet needs from the least painful to the most painful. Then on the right side, list the most relevant or applicable memory related to that need.

Unmet Need	Memory

INDIVIDUAL HEARTWORK – PARTS OF SELF

1. Identify an emotional struggle you recently experienced and describe the struggle below.

2. How old (or young) did you feel emotionally in the moment?

3. Now draw or describe below the parts of self that were activated within this struggle and what these parts were saying and feeling.

    a. The child that acts out:

b. The overbearing inner critic:

c. The highly vulnerable and wounded child:

Identify a second emotional struggle that you recently experienced and describe the struggle below.

How old (or young) did you feel emotionally in the moment?

Now draw or describe below the parts of self that were activated within this struggle and what these parts were saying and feeling.

The child that acts out:

The overbearing inner critic:

The highly vulnerable and wounded child:

QUADRUPLE ENTRY JOURNALING™ OVERVIEW

We will utilize Quadruple Entry Journaling™ for each unmet need memory listed in your **Ordering Unmet Needs Memories**. Our approach will be to address the memories from least to most painful, knowing that even addressing one memory at a time can initiate the rewiring of our neural networks. It is not necessary to address every memory, rather, we want to focus on the most impactful memories from each theme. This will allow us to establish restorative experiences and create the "heart home" God intended for us.

As we allow our child parts to express their emotions, we will use our holy imagination to welcome Jesus into our memories of unmet needs. Additionally, we will use our Self-Momming™ tool and imagine the presence of safe others. You can always go back and work on the less impactful memories at a later time.

Furthermore, we will be using the power of mental imagery to facilitate this process. Studies have shown that mental imagery has a significant impact on both behavioral and brain imaging studies, with the brain perceiving imagined experiences in a similar way to actual experiences. This can lead to transformation in one's internal representations of self and the world.[4]

By utilizing our holy imagination, our psyche will register, and our child parts will receive nurturing, which will transform our heart home. God desires to restore our lives and give us back seven times more than what the enemy stole (Proverbs 6:31).

Yet when he is found, he must restore sevenfold;
He may have to give up all the substance of his house.

Proverbs 6:31 (NKJV)

His love and mercy toward us are boundless, and this process will allow us to experience His restoration and healing in a tangible way.

INDIVIDUAL HEARTWORK QUADRUPLE ENTRY JOURNALING™

As mentioned in the above overview, work on each memory one at a time starting with your least painful memory.

Memory. You will describe your memory in column one. Write about your memory in as much detail as you can remember, spending time thinking about it and accessing your child parts' feelings about it. This will help to open a Memory Reconsolidation window so that emotional learning can be shifted.

Unmet Needs. Next, use the below list of unmet needs to identify and report on your unmet needs within the memory with which you are working in column one.

Acceptance	Guidance
Adequate nutrition	Opportunities for growth
Acknowledgement	Model of Self-control
Body Respect	Nurture
Belonging	Order in home
Boundaries	Peaceful family environment
Comfort	Physical health
Compassion	Physical safety
Connection	Predictability
Consistency	Protection
Healthy communication	Proper autonomy
Healthy connection	Recognition
Healthy friendships	Rules
Honesty	Self-expression
Honor toward sexuality	Sense of competence
Empathy	Sense of control
Emotional safety	Sense of identity
Emotional security	Sense of purpose
Encouragement	Sense of worth
Fairness (no favoritism)	Understanding
Fun	

Child Part Feelings. In column two, you will write your feelings in the memory from the point of view of your younger child parts. You may experience parts of self that are afraid and other parts that are angry. You may even experience parts that feel shame and false guilt. False guilt is a common emotional response to trauma that may lead a person to feel responsible or at fault for something not within their control, such as the actions of others or the circumstances of a traumatic event. List all your feelings. Do not limit yourself to the provided list below; include any other feelings that arise.

Abandonment	Hypervigilance
Anger	Impulsivity
Anxiety	Intrusion
Apathy	Isolation
Avoidance	Jealousy
Betrayal	Loneliness
Bitterness	Loss of control
Confusion	Numbness
Despair	Pain
Desperation	Panic
Detachment	Pleasure
Disgust	Powerlessness
Distrust	Regret
Dissociation	Relief
Embarrassment	Rejection
Envy	Resentment
Fear	Sadness
Flashbacks	Self-blame
Frustration	Self-doubt
Grief	Self-hatred
Guilt	Shame
Helplessness	Startled
Hopelessness	Suicidal
Hyperactivity	Targeted
Hyperarousal	Vulnerability

Take time to explore and sit with the emotions you listed in column two. Use your Tracking skill to curiously attend to the sensations in your body as you revisit the memory. If these emotions and sensations had a color or texture, what would they be? Observe how they move and shift, as you lovingly attend to them. This will help open a Memory Reconsolidation window and allow for emotional learning to shift.

However, it is important to stay within your Window of Tolerance. If you start to feel overwhelmed and notice yourself moving toward a fight, flight, or freeze response, put down this activity and use your RESOURCE™ tools to regulate your emotions. Once you feel more grounded, you can come back to the exercise.

Spend time in prayer and ask the Lord, "What do You want to show me within this memory?" Use Pneumaception™ to hear, see, and sense what He is wanting to say. Remember that Jesus is the giver of life, as John 10:10 (NIV) tells us, "The thief comes only to steal and kill and destroy; I have come that they may have life, and have it to the full."

As you wait on the Lord, keep in mind James 1:17 (KJV), which reminds us that, "Every good and perfect gift is from above, coming down from the Father of the heavenly lights, who does not change like shifting shadows." Trust that whatever Jesus shows you in this memory, He is always good and perfect.

It is also important to be aware of the devil's activity, as John 8:44 (NIV) tells us, "He was a murderer from the beginning, not holding to the truth, for there is no truth in him. When he lies, he speaks his native language, for he is a liar and the father of lies." If any thoughts or feelings arise that bring death or destruction, know they are not from Jesus, but rather from the enemy. Ask Jesus to reveal the truth and to bring healing to any areas that have been impacted by the enemy's lies.

As we encounter Jesus in our memories, He brings life, hope, comfort, safety, and security. He wants to meet the need that was not met in your early life. Allow Jesus to meet every unmet need. Ask Him, "Jesus show me how YOU meet my need of _____." Then, watch and listen with your spirit eyes and ears. He is the restorer of all things lost.

Remember, you are His sheep, so you hear His voice. Sometimes, what Jesus says is so good, it is hard to believe. He is the Good Shepard, and you can believe His personal words of life to you. Write down all He shows you.

Self Momming™. In column four, we will use our Self-Momming™ skill to provide comfort, love, and nurture to our younger parts affected by the memory. We will write a letter to our younger selves, reassuring those parts they are loved, valued, and protected. We will tell them what they needed to hear at that time and provide the care they deserved. We will also use our imagination to visualize holding

and soothing our younger selves, meeting every need. This will help to provide a sense of safety and security that was missing during the traumatic experience. Remember, we have power within through our connection with Jesus to provide ourselves with the love and care we needed, but may not have received at the time.

If you struggle with anxious or disorganized attachment, this step may feel daunting, but it is crucial. By practicing Self-Momming™, we are taking a step toward healing our relationship with our vulnerable parts. If you find it difficult to love your inner child, try to imagine a child in your life who shares similar traits and meditate on their inherent lovability. Then, turn that same kindness and compassion toward your inner child. Ask Jesus to help you see yourself through His eyes and to love yourself as He loves you.

Receiving from Safe Others. In column five, we go back to the memory, still bringing in Jesus and Self-Momming™, and we also add in safe others. Here you can again be lavish in using your holy imagination. For example, if your husband or adult sister is a safe person in your life, you can bring them back into the memory at current age. Place all the support from others you can in your memory and imagine them, with Jesus and Self as Mom meeting your little one's every need. In column five, write down how your needs were met.

If you struggle with avoidant or disorganized attachment, this step may feel intimidating, but it is necessary. Your temptation may be to shy away from leaning on others. God made us to need others, and part of your healing is to allow safe others in to support you. Ask Jesus to help you see others through His eyes and to help you to feel safe in letting others support you.

Now it is time for you to do the work in your own heart home. Complete your Quadruple Entry Journaling™ below. Make sure you work through all key memories.

Memory and Unmet Needs- Describe	Child Part Feelings:	Encounter with Jesus- let Him meet your needs	Self-Mom-ming™: Meet your needs as a mother would	Receiving from Safe Others: al-low others to meet your needs
Memory 1: Unmet Needs:				

Memory and Unmet Needs-Describe	Child Part Feelings:	Encounter with Jesus-let Him meet your needs	Self-Momming™: Meet your needs as a mother would	Receiving from Safe Others: allow others to meet your needs
Memory 2: Unmet Needs:				

Memory and Unmet Needs- Describe	Child Part Feelings:	Encounter with Jesus- let Him meet your needs	Self-Mom-ming™: Meet your needs as a mother would	Receiving from Safe Others: al-low others to meet your needs
Memory 3: Unmet Needs:				

Memory and Unmet Needs- Describe	Child Part Feelings:	Encounter with Jesus- let Him meet your needs	Self-Mom- ming™: Meet your needs as a mother would	Receiving from Safe Others: al- low others to meet your needs
Memory 4: Unmet Needs:				

Memory and Unmet Needs- Describe	Child Part Feelings:	Encounter with Jesus- let Him meet your needs	Self-Mom-ming™: Meet your needs as a mother would	Receiving from Safe Others: al-low others to meet your needs
Memory 5: Unmet Needs:				

Memory and Unmet Needs- Describe	Child Part Feelings:	Encounter with Jesus- let Him meet your needs	Self-Mom-ming™: Meet your needs as a mother would	Receiving from Safe Others: al-low others to meet your needs
Memory 6: Unmet Needs:				

Memory and Unmet Needs- Describe	Child Part Feelings:	Encounter with Jesus- let Him meet your needs	Self-Mom-ming™: Meet your needs as a mother would	Receiving from Safe Others: al-low others to meet your needs
Memory 7: Unmet Needs:				

Memory and Unmet Needs-Describe	Child Part Feelings:	Encounter with Jesus-let Him meet your needs	Self-Mom-ming™: Meet your needs as a mother would	Receiving from Safe Others: allow others to meet your needs
Memory 8: Unmet Needs:				

Memory and Unmet Needs- Describe	Child Part Feelings:	Encounter with Jesus- let Him meet your needs	Self-Mom-ming™: Meet your needs as a mother would	Receiving from Safe Others: al-low others to meet your needs
Memory 9: Unmet Needs:				

Memory and Unmet Needs- Describe	Child Part Feelings:	Encounter with Jesus- let Him meet your needs	Self-Momming™: Meet your needs as a mother would	Receiving from Safe Others: allow others to meet your needs
Memory 10: Unmet Needs:				

INDIVIDUAL HEARTWORK – STICKY MEMORIES

Write down the Sticky Memories that remained unmoved or stuck after your above work.

INDIVIDUAL HEARTWORK – OSCILLATION WITH JESUS™ ACTIVITY

Oscillation with Jesus™ is a powerful tool we use to process and resolve unmet needs from Sticky Memories. It can also be used to process trauma triggers. It involves following an imaginal figure-eight with a positive and negative stimulus associated with the trauma. We spend more time on the positive side and gradually gain a tolerance for expanding our time on the negative side as the trigger loses negative emotional valence. We will use a safe and belonging-filled memory with Jesus on the right side of the figure-eight and your Sticky Memory on the left. This technique helps us integrate new, positive emotional learning into the memory and reduce the emotional distress associated with it.

Begin by finding a comfortable position, either sitting or lying down. Take a deep breath in and slowly release it. Close your eyes and focus your attention on your breath, breathing in the life of God, exhaling stress.

Now, use your holy imagination to envision an invisible figure-eight in the air in front of you. Position it horizontally so the loops are facing left and right. The right loop represents a safe and belonging-filled memory with Jesus, while the left loop represents your Sticky Memory or Trauma Trigger.

As we start tracing the figure-eight, focus on the right loop, the safe memory with Jesus. Think about a highly positive image associated with this memory. It could be a place, a situation, or a feeling. Spend a few moments here, soaking in this positive sensation.

Now, as we trace the left loop, think about the trigger you want to defuse. Be mindful of your emotions and stay within a manageable emotional zone, your Window of Tolerance. Spend less time on this side at the beginning, and slowly expand as the trigger loses its negative emotional valence.

Keep looping back and forth, spending more time on the positive side and gradually expanding your time on the negative side as negative emotions decrease. As you do this, observe how your body feels when exposed to both sides of the Oscillation.

Remember, Jesus is with you throughout this process. You are not alone. Keep breathing and tracing the figure-eight with your imagination, letting the Oscillation tool discharge and reconsolidate the Trigger.

When you are ready, take a deep breath in and slowly release it. Open your eyes and take a moment to ground yourself before resuming your study.

Use this QR code to access audible versions of activities.

Write about your experience with Oscillation with Jesus™ below.

INDIVIDUAL HEARTWORK – PAIN TO PURPOSE DRAWING™

Drawing One: Pain. For your first drawing, you will draw the felt sense of the Sticky Memory. In other words, if you could express the feeling you have within the memory through drawing, what would you draw? I am not asking you to draw the memory, but the feeling.

Whatever comes to you is fine, just start drawing how you feel. In addition, remain in a non-judgmental attitude as you draw, as most of us are not artists. The important part is to draw your felt sense in the memory. After you work on drawing one, check in with your body. What are you feeling? Honor these feelings.

Drawing Two: Opposite. For your second drawing, you will look at Drawing One and draw the opposite for Drawing Two. If you were to draw the opposite of the feeling of Drawing One, what would you draw? Ponder this, and draw whatever image comes to you. Remember, do not judge your drawing abilities. The important action is to draw the opposite of the first picture. After you work on drawing two, check in with your body. What are you feeling? Honor these feelings. Ponder, how can I create more of these positive feelings?

Drawing Three: Kingdom Purpose. Next, we will use the Heart Journey Beautiful Place Prayer™. Ask the Lord, "What do You want to do with this pain to transform it into a Beautiful Place"? The Lord wants to take our wounded places, heal them, and use them for His purpose. Sit before Him and use Pneumaception™. Once He speaks to you, draw what He shows you. Notice the hope and Kingdom purpose in what He showed you. Allow hope to fill your heart as an anchor of your soul (Hebrews 6:19).

Memory #1: List the Unmet Need memory with which you will work.

Draw three drawings according to the directions above.

Drawing One: Pain

Drawing Two: Opposite

Drawing Three: Kingdom Purpose

Memory #2: List the Unmet Need memory with which you will work.

Draw three drawings according to the directions above.

Drawing One: Pain

Drawing Two: Opposite

Drawing Three: Kingdom Purpose

Memory #3: List the Unmet Need memory with which you will work.

Draw three drawings according to the directions above.

Drawing One: Pain

Drawing Two: Opposite

Drawing Three: Kingdom Purpose

Memory #4: List the Unmet Need memory with which you will work.

Draw three drawings according to the directions above.

Drawing One: Pain

Drawing Two: Opposite

Drawing Three: Kingdom Purpose

INDIVIDUAL HEARTWORK BEAUTIFUL PLACE PRAYER™ ACTIVITY

In this activity, go to the Lord in a Beautiful Place and surrender your pain. Ask Him to show you how He can turn it into something beautiful. Trust God through the Beautiful Place Prayer™ and ask Him to use your story to bring hope and comfort to others.

1. Describe your Beautiful Place Prayer below:

2. What pain did you give Him?

3. Write out a prayer, asking Him to turn your pain into something beautiful:

INDIVIDUAL HEARTWORK EMPTY CHAIR – CHRISTIAN VERSION ACTIVITY

The Empty Chair - Christian Version involves imagining the person sitting in an empty chair across from you, then using your voice to express how their actions affected you.

To make this intervention even more powerful, you will invite Jesus to stand with you as you boldly express your feelings to the person in the chair. You can ask Him to help you find the right words to say and to give you the strength and courage you need to speak your truth.

In addition to Jesus, you will Self-Mom, imagining yourself as your own loving mother offering support, validation and encouragement as you speak to the person in the chair. This technique will help you feel safer and more supported as you work through your feelings. You can also invite safe others, a "cloud of witnesses," to surround you with love and support. This technique can help you heal old wounds, release pent-up emotions, and move forward with greater clarity and peace.

Find a comfortable seated position, close your eyes and take a deep breath in imagining that you are breathing in the life of God, and slowly exhale. Allow yourself to relax, and let go of any tension or stress you may be feeling.

As you begin to imagine an empty chair in front of you, invite Jesus to stand with you. Ask Him to help you find the right words to say, to give you the strength and courage you need to speak your truth. Visualize Him standing by your side, with His loving and supportive presence.

As you speak to the person in the chair, imagine that they can hear you loud and clear. With Jesus standing beside you, helping you find the right words to say, the person in the chair will receive what you say. As you express your feelings and how their actions impacted you, feel the weight being lifted off your soul.

In addition to Jesus, you will Self-Mom™, imagining yourself as your own loving mother offering support, validation, and encouragement as you speak to the person in the chair. This technique will help you feel safer and more supported as you work through your feelings. You can also invite safe others, a "cloud of witnesses," to surround you with love and support.

When you are ready, wiggle your fingers and toes, and slowly open your eyes if they were closed. Soften into the love of Jesus and the power of your voice. Remember, you were meant to be heard.

Use this QR code to access audible versions of activities.

INDIVIDUAL HEARTWORK – EMPTY CHAIR – CHRISTIAN VERSION

Now journal about your experience in Empty Chair - Christian Version.

RESTORED CHILDHOOD WITH JESUS ACTIVITY

The Restored Childhood with Jesus Activity is a transformative tool that utilizes your holy imagination to help you encounter Jesus. He will meet the unmet needs from your childhood as you allow Jesus to restore and fill the gaps of your childhood experiences.

To fully immerse yourself in this activity, use Scripture as your guide and the sword of the Spirit. Speak the words of Ephesians 3:20 (NIV) to your heart, "Now to Him who is able to do immeasurably more than all we ask or imagine according to His power that has worked within us." Pay attention to the word "imagine" and allow yourself to fully understand, think, consider, apprehend, and even realize the limitless possibilities of His goodness touching every aspect of your childhood and life.

Repeat this activity as many times as necessary, using your holy imagination to experience the love and restoration of Jesus in every unmet need from your childhood. Allow His power to work within you and bring healing and wholeness to your heart and soul.

INDIVIDUAL HEARTWORK – RESTORED CHILDHOOD WITH JESUS ACTIVITY

To begin this activity, find somewhere comfortable. Feel your back and bottom and the rest of your body being supported. During this activity, we will use your holy imagination and invite God into an experience where you can have what God intended for all of us to have—being born into a home with parents who were ready to parent us and give us that opportunity for secure attachment.

As you get comfortable, your eyes open or closed, take a deep breath and know the Lord is with you.

Try to imagine what it might be like for your mom and dad, several years before you were born, to have some changes in their lives, where their needs were significantly met— where their needs were addressed in a whole new way, where they could really experience life in a different way. Imagine the Lord providing this for them.

Imagine your mom receiving what she needed. Imagine the Lord orchestrating events where your mom had what she needed to be an exceptional mother to you. Maybe, in your imagination, she had community, a church filled with loving, honest, sincere, fun Christian women who reached out to her. Maybe she had a psychotherapist or a psychologist helping her.

Imagine the same for your father, having all he needs to be an amazing father. Imagine that both your parents have had interventions before your birth so that they were able to grow in areas to prepare for you. They are opening up their hearts in ways we can only imagine, and the Lord is doing this for you. Just allow yourself to experience this, thinking about them with whole hearts.

As time goes on, their love for one another and the Lord grows. Imagine them dreaming of you and creating you in love. My friend, you were made to be created in love. It is God's intention. Imagine yourself growing in a womb that is completely safe, free from any outside harm, where you are nurtured and knit together by your Heavenly

Father. Imagine the Holy Spirit aligning every piece of your DNA to make you just how you need to be.

Our Heavenly Father put you together, just how you are supposed to be, wonderfully and fearfully made. Imagine a safe womb environment where you are growing and being put together free from harm. Also imagine your mother, in a peaceful state of bliss as she anticipates your birth. You are not absorbing any stress hormones, just the goodness of the Lord, as the Lord intended it.

Now imagine it is time for you to be born. Where would you like to be born? We are going give you a new welcome into the world the way the Lord intended for you.

Imagine the people you want to be there as you are born and come into this world. In this activity, you are welcome to invite whomever you want into your birthing experience. Do you want to be born outside or inside of a hospital? Regardless, you are getting the most exquisite love, attention, and care, coming into this world safely and in a safe emotional attachment scenario. Your parents have every need met, being established in whatever careers they wanted, along with plenty of food in the cupboards and love in the heart. The Lord is with all of you.

And now, imagine it is time for you to go home for the first time. What should that be like? Being welcomed into the home, maybe by siblings, aunts, and uncles, knowing the Lord is there and supporting you. He is the glue holding the family together. And you are a part of that. There is freedom for you to just be who you are in this family. Imagine the Lord continuing to meet your parents' needs as you continue to grow and become a toddler, then a preschooler. Your parents are so proud of you, hanging your artwork on the fridge. The Lord is hanging your artwork on the fridge, too.

As you grow, your parents are providing the right boundaries so you can explore, but have a safe place to go back to. And, you are protected, when you need to be protected. You are free to play because you don't have to watch your back because they are—your mother, father, and the Lord.

As you move into elementary school, imagine your loving parents at every award ceremony and helping you through every struggle, rejoicing with you in every joy. Envision them helping you through the peer problems and troubles, and taking wonderful family vacations. How does that feel in your body?

Imagine being in this family, where every need is met, and imagine your parents having every need met. What does that feel like?

Allow yourself to soften into this experience, through each part of your body—your legs, arms, stomach, shoulders, head, and face—even if part of you wants to shy away from it. Come back and allow yourself to experience this.

Moving on to middle school, experience your parents being there for all those talks you need and giving you grace when you slam the door. They help you through challenges with your peers and help you succeed in all your activities.

While you are in high school, imagine your parents being what you need them to be, both with boundaries and secure attachment. You are so very loved.

And imagine yourself launching into life with this amazing new sense of home and sense of belonging in your heart. Feel that belonging you have with the Lord and with your family, as they have had every need met and are able to create that sense of belonging in the family environment. Let yourself lavish in that sense of belonging your heart has longed for. It is time to give yourself the gift of that belonging and growing up to have that sense of belonging in your friend groups, with your siblings, knowing everything is okay. Allow yourself that felt sense in your body that you belong to the Lord and to a family who loves you.

Maybe that was your experience, in part. Maybe you did not have very much of that, but it is time for you to allow yourself to use your imagination to receive this experience that the Lord wants you to have so He can heal your heart.

Beloved, allow more comfort on the inside, drinking in more of His love, and more of that belonging and healing even right now, in Jesus' name.

Use this QR code to access audible versions of activities.

INDIVIDUAL HEARTWORK – RESTORED CHILDHOOD WITH JESUS

Reflect on your experience during the Individual Heartwork - Restored Childhood with Jesus Activity.

1. What emotions and thoughts did you experience during the activity?

2. How did it feel to imagine your parents and family in this ideal situation?

3. Were there any difficult emotions that came up for you during the activity, and if so, what were they and how did you manage them?

4. Reflect on the impact this meditation activity had on you, and consider how you can use this experience to further your healing and growth.

5. Finally, write about any insights or revelations you gained during the activity that you can apply to your life moving forward.

INDIVIDUAL HEARTWORK – CHILDHOOD LOSSES AND UNCOVERED GRIEF

Write a letter to your inner child, inviting Jesus to be present with you and your younger self as you acknowledge any pain and losses that were experienced. Allow Jesus to offer words of affirmation, comfort, and hope to your inner child, as if He were speaking directly to them. Take as much time as you need to fully express your emotions and allow Jesus to minister to your heart. How does this exercise make you feel? Is there anything else that Jesus may want to say to your inner child?

INDIVIDUAL HEARTWORK – CHAPTER SIX REVIEW

Reflect on and journal your answers to the below questions:

1.   How did it feel to work through each unmet need?

2.   Now, consider how you feel after inviting the Lord into that experience or area of your life. Journal how your mind, heart, and body responded in a positive way.

3.   In what ways do you feel this Heartwork will help you in tough situations in the future?

4. When an unmet need from childhood is triggered, how can you use the tools in this lesson to address it?

5. If you had one thing to remember that Jesus pressed on your heart as you went through this lesson, what would it be?

HEART GROUP DISCUSSION – TIME TO SHARE.

1. As you prayed and went through this lesson, which Scripture did God reveal to you to support you in this phase of the journey? Share with your group or safe person why this particular Scripture resonates with you and how you plan to integrate it into your healing.

2. How did you feel at the beginning of this lesson before allowing the Lord to work with your unmet needs?

3. How do you feel now after inviting the Lord into those broken and mildewed parts of your heart home?

4. As you continue on this Heart Journey™, share with your group and/or prayer and accountability partner how you intend to address your critical self when she tries to disrupt that renovated part of your heart.

5. To this point, you have addressed a lot of painful memories and trauma. Be authentic with your small group sisters and/or prayer and accountability partner. Share how they can help support you in this phase of your Heart Journey™.

Keystone Scriptures for Restoring My Emotions

NOW MEMORIZE THESE KEYSTONE SCRIPTURES:

My father and mother abandoned me.
But You, Yahweh, took me in and made me Yours.

Psalm 27:10 (TPT)

Even when Your path takes me through
the valley of deepest darkness,
fear will never conquer me, for You already have!
Your authority is my strength and my peace.
The comfort of Your love takes away my fear.
I'll never be lonely, for You are near.

Psalm 23:4 (TPT)

…be entwined as one with the Lord.

Psalm 27:14b (TPT)

You satisfy my every desire with good things.
You've supercharged my life so that I soar again
like a flying eagle in the sky!

Psalm 103:5 (TPT)

LET US PRAY.

Heavenly Father, we come before You with grateful hearts, asking for Your healing touch upon our hearts and memories. Lord, we pray that You would go into every nook and cranny of our heart homes, removing everything the enemy intended for evil and replacing it with Your love, acceptance, belonging, wholeness, and healing. We pray for freedom from the chains that bind us and speak freedom in the mighty name of Jesus.

Holy Spirit, we invite You into this place, blessing and making Yourself at home. We ask that You renovate and reconstruct our hearts and memories, pouring out Your Spirit upon us. Lord, we pray that there would be no space left unturned or unhealed in our memories. Meet every need, Lord, and heal every space in our hearts.

Father, we thank You that right now, hearts are being healed and receiving You in new ways. We welcome You into every room, every corner, and every storage space of our hearts. We pray that there would be no distance between us and You in any space. Thank You for seeking out every lost place within us, like the woman who had nine coins but looked for the one lost one.

Lord, we thank You that every part of ourselves comes to the table, just like Mephibosheth ate at the king's table. We thank You for continuing this healing work and for adopting each part of each person to Yourself, joining them to their forever home in You.

In Jesus' name, Amen.

Chapter

SEVEN

RESTORING MY SECURITY

You will keep in perfect and constant peace the one whose mind is steadfast [that is, committed and focused on You—in both inclination and character], Because He trusts and takes refuge in You [with hope and confident expectation].

Isaiah 26:3 (AMP)

SUPPLIES

For this chapter's Heartwork, you will need a pen or pencil and your *Heart Journey™ Journal.* As you engage with your chapter seven Heartwork, you will also need pen or pencil, colored pencils or markers for drawing, and your list of "Traumas" from your chapter five timelines.

INDIVIDUAL HEARTWORK – ORDERING TRAUMAS

Return to your Heartwork from Chapter Five, and find your list of traumas. List your traumas from the least painful to the most painful.

Traumas

INDIVIDUAL HEARTWORK – FROM ALONE TO CONNECTION

List the safe people you will want to use in your trauma work. Remember, we are using your holy imagination to meet the needs of your most vulnerable self, so we want Jesus and Self as Mom™ on the list. In addition, you can have anyone else present in the memories. Be creative! Moreover, you can integrate in angels and other heavenly beings! Allow lavish support as you rework your trauma memories.

INDIVIDUAL HEARTWORK – TIME REVERSE TRAUMA™

1. Description of Trauma #1:

2. When did you know it was over?

3. What does it feel like in your body to know it is over?

4. Identify an image that represents that "it [this trauma] is over" to use in your trauma work:

5. Who do you want with you now in this trauma?

6. Work with your trauma, starting with T-7 (or T-5 if you want to break the trauma into fewer "slices"). Also, complete T+7 (or T+5 if you want to break the trauma into fewer "slices"). Work from T-7 to T+7, completing each block (what happened, resource you want there to help you through it, response that you need to complete regarding fight, flight, etc.). Use your holy imagination to see and feel each need being met.

T-7 (Before I know the trauma was coming)	T-6	T-5
Write or draw what did happen:	Write or draw what did happen:	Write or draw what did happen:
What resource do you want here?	What resource do you want here?	What resource do you want here?
What response(s) needs to be completed:	What response(s) needs to be completed:	What response(s) needs to be completed:
T-4	T-3	T-2
Write or draw what did happen:	Write or draw what did happen:	Write or draw what did happen:
What resource do you want here?	What resource do you want here?	What resource do you want here?
What response(s) needs to be completed:	What response(s) needs to be completed:	What response(s) needs to be completed:

Heart Journey

T-1	T-0 (Before I know the trauma was coming)	T+1
Write or draw what did happen:	Write or draw what did happen:	Write or draw what did happen:
What resource do you want here?	What resource do you want here?	What resource do you want here?
What response(s) needs to be completed:	What response(s) needs to be completed:	What response(s) needs to be completed:
T+2	T+3	T+4
Write or draw what did happen:	Write or draw what did happen:	Write or draw what did happen:
What resource do you want here?	What resource do you want here?	What resource do you want here?
What response(s) needs to be completed:	What response(s) needs to be completed:	What response(s) needs to be completed:

Restoring My Security

T+5 (Before I know the trauma was coming)	T+6	T+7 (Before I know the trauma was coming)
Write or draw what did happen:	**Write or draw what did happen:**	**Write or draw what did happen:**
What resource do you want here?	**What resource do you want here?**	**What resource do you want here?**
What response(s) needs to be completed:	**What response(s) needs to be completed:**	**What response(s) needs to be completed:**

1. Description of Trauma #2:

2. When did you know it was over?

3. What does it feel like in your body to know it is over?

4. Identify an image that represents that "it [this trauma] is over" to use in your trauma work:

5. Who do you want with you now in this trauma?

6. Work with your trauma, starting with T-7 (or T-5 if you want to break the trauma into fewer "slices"). Also, complete T+7 (or T+5 if you want to break the trauma into fewer "slices"). Work from T-7 to T+7, completing each block (what happened, resource you want there to help you through it, response that you need to complete regarding fight, flight, etc.). Use your holy imagination to see and feel each need being met.

T-7 (Before I know the trauma was coming)	T-6	T-5
Write or draw what did happen:	Write or draw what did happen:	Write or draw what did happen:
What resource do you want here?	What resource do you want here?	What resource do you want here?
What response(s) needs to be completed:	What response(s) needs to be completed:	What response(s) needs to be completed:
T-4	T-3	T-2
Write or draw what did happen:	Write or draw what did happen:	Write or draw what did happen:
What resource do you want here?	What resource do you want here?	What resource do you want here?
What response(s) needs to be completed:	What response(s) needs to be completed:	What response(s) needs to be completed:

T-1	T-0 (Before I know the trauma was coming)	T+1
Write or draw what did happen:	Write or draw what did happen:	Write or draw what did happen:
What resource do you want here?	What resource do you want here?	What resource do you want here?
What response(s) needs to be completed:	What response(s) needs to be completed:	What response(s) needs to be completed:
T+2	T+3	T+4
Write or draw what did happen:	Write or draw what did happen:	Write or draw what did happen:
What resource do you want here?	What resource do you want here?	What resource do you want here?
What response(s) needs to be completed:	What response(s) needs to be completed:	What response(s) needs to be completed:

T+5 (Before I know the trauma was coming)	T+6	T+7 (Before I know the trauma was coming)
Write or draw what did happen:	Write or draw what did happen:	Write or draw what did happen:
What resource do you want here?	What resource do you want here?	What resource do you want here?
What response(s) needs to be completed:	What response(s) needs to be completed:	What response(s) needs to be completed:

1. Description of Trauma #3:

2. When did you know it was over?

3. What does it feel like in your body to know it is over?

4. Identify an image that represents that "it [this trauma] is over" to use in your trauma work:

5. Who do you want with you now in this trauma?

6. Work with your trauma, starting with T-7 (or T-5 if you want to break the trauma into fewer "slices"). Also, complete T+7 (or T+5 if you want to break the trauma into fewer "slices"). Work from T-7 to T+7, completing each block (what happened, resource you want there to help you through it, response that you need to complete regarding fight, flight, etc.). Use your holy imagination to see and feel each need being met.

Restoring My Security

T-7 (Before I know the trauma was coming)	T-6	T-5
Write or draw what did happen:	Write or draw what did happen:	Write or draw what did happen:
What resource do you want here?	What resource do you want here?	What resource do you want here?
What response(s) needs to be completed:	What response(s) needs to be completed:	What response(s) needs to be completed:
T-4	T-3	T-2
Write or draw what did happen:	Write or draw what did happen:	Write or draw what did happen:
What resource do you want here?	What resource do you want here?	What resource do you want here?
What response(s) needs to be completed:	What response(s) needs to be completed:	What response(s) needs to be completed:

T-1	T-0 (Before I know the trauma was coming)	T+1
Write or draw what did happen:	Write or draw what did happen:	Write or draw what did happen:
What resource do you want here?	What resource do you want here?	What resource do you want here?
What response(s) needs to be completed:	What response(s) needs to be completed:	What response(s) needs to be completed:
T+2	T+3	T+4
Write or draw what did happen:	Write or draw what did happen:	Write or draw what did happen:
What resource do you want here?	What resource do you want here?	What resource do you want here?
What response(s) needs to be completed:	What response(s) needs to be completed:	What response(s) needs to be completed:

Restoring My Security

T+5 (Before I know the trauma was coming)	T+6	T+7 (Before I know the trauma was coming)
Write or draw what did happen:	**Write or draw what did happen:**	**Write or draw what did happen:**
What resource do you want here?	**What resource do you want here?**	**What resource do you want here?**
What response(s) needs to be completed:	**What response(s) needs to be completed:**	**What response(s) needs to be completed:**

1. Description of Trauma #4:

2. When did you know it was over?

3. What does it feel like in your body to know it is over?

4. Identify an image that represents that "it [this trauma] is over" to use in your trauma work:

5. Who do you want with you now in this trauma?

6. Work with your trauma, starting with T-7 (or T-5 if you want to break the trauma into fewer "slices"). Also, complete T+7 (or T+5 if you want to break the trauma into fewer "slices"). Work from T-7 to T+7, completing each block (what happened, resource you want there to help you through it, response that you need to complete regarding fight, flight, etc.). Use your holy imagination to see and feel each need being met.

T-7 (Before I know the trauma was coming)	T-6	T-5
Write or draw what did happen:	Write or draw what did happen:	Write or draw what did happen:
What resource do you want here?	What resource do you want here?	What resource do you want here?
What response(s) needs to be completed:	What response(s) needs to be completed:	What response(s) needs to be completed:
T-4	T-3	T-2
Write or draw what did happen:	Write or draw what did happen:	Write or draw what did happen:
What resource do you want here?	What resource do you want here?	What resource do you want here?
What response(s) needs to be completed:	What response(s) needs to be completed:	What response(s) needs to be completed:

T-1	T-0 (Before I know the trauma was coming)	T+1
Write or draw what did happen:	Write or draw what did happen:	Write or draw what did happen:
What resource do you want here?	What resource do you want here?	What resource do you want here?
What response(s) needs to be completed:	What response(s) needs to be completed:	What response(s) needs to be completed:
T+2	T+3	T+4
Write or draw what did happen:	Write or draw what did happen:	Write or draw what did happen:
What resource do you want here?	What resource do you want here?	What resource do you want here?
What response(s) needs to be completed:	What response(s) needs to be completed:	What response(s) needs to be completed:

Restoring My Security

T+5 (Before I know the trauma was coming)	T+6	T+7 (Before I know the trauma was coming)
Write or draw what did happen:	Write or draw what did happen:	Write or draw what did happen:
What resource do you want here?	What resource do you want here?	What resource do you want here?
What response(s) needs to be completed:	What response(s) needs to be completed:	What response(s) needs to be completed:

1. Description of Trauma #5:

2. When did you know it was over?

3. What does it feel like in your body to know it is over?

4. Identify an image that represents that "it [this trauma] is over" to use in your trauma work:

5. Who do you want with you now in this trauma?

6. Work with your trauma, starting with T-7 (or T-5 if you want to break the trauma into fewer "slices"). Also, complete T+7 (or T+5 if you want to break the trauma into fewer "slices"). Work from T-7 to T+7, completing each block (what happened, resource you want there to help you through it, response that you need to complete regarding fight, flight, etc.). Use your holy imagination to see and feel each need being met.

T-7 (Before I know the trauma was coming)	T-6	T-5
Write or draw what did happen:	Write or draw what did happen:	Write or draw what did happen:
What resource do you want here?	What resource do you want here?	What resource do you want here?
What response(s) needs to be completed:	What response(s) needs to be completed:	What response(s) needs to be completed:
T-4	T-3	T-2
Write or draw what did happen:	Write or draw what did happen:	Write or draw what did happen:
What resource do you want here?	What resource do you want here?	What resource do you want here?
What response(s) needs to be completed:	What response(s) needs to be completed:	What response(s) needs to be completed:

T-1	T-0 (Before I know the trauma was coming)	T+1
Write or draw what did happen:	Write or draw what did happen:	Write or draw what did happen:
What resource do you want here?	What resource do you want here?	What resource do you want here?
What response(s) needs to be completed:	What response(s) needs to be completed:	What response(s) needs to be completed:
T+2	T+3	T+4
Write or draw what did happen:	Write or draw what did happen:	Write or draw what did happen:
What resource do you want here?	What resource do you want here?	What resource do you want here?
What response(s) needs to be completed:	What response(s) needs to be completed:	What response(s) needs to be completed:

Restoring My Security

T+5 (Before I know the trauma was coming)	T+6	T+7 (Before I know the trauma was coming)
Write or draw what did happen:	Write or draw what did happen:	Write or draw what did happen:
What resource do you want here?	What resource do you want here?	What resource do you want here?
What response(s) needs to be completed:	What response(s) needs to be completed:	What response(s) needs to be completed:

1. Description of Trauma #6:

2. When did you know it was over?

3. What does it feel like in your body to know it is over?

4. Identify an image that represents that "it [this trauma] is over" to use in your trauma work:

5. Who do you want with you now in this trauma?

6. Work with your trauma, starting with T-7 (or T-5 if you want to break the trauma into fewer "slices"). Also, complete T+7 (or T+5 if you want to break the trauma into fewer "slices"). Work from T-7 to T+7, completing each block (what happened, resource you want there to help you through it, response that you need to complete regarding fight, flight, etc.). Use your holy imagination to see and feel each need being met.

Restoring My Security

T-7 (Before I know the trauma was coming)	T-6	T-5
Write or draw what did happen:	Write or draw what did happen:	Write or draw what did happen:
What resource do you want here?	What resource do you want here?	What resource do you want here?
What response(s) needs to be completed:	What response(s) needs to be completed:	What response(s) needs to be completed:
T-4	T-3	T-2
Write or draw what did happen:	Write or draw what did happen:	Write or draw what did happen:
What resource do you want here?	What resource do you want here?	What resource do you want here?
What response(s) needs to be completed:	What response(s) needs to be completed:	What response(s) needs to be completed:

T-1	T-0 (Before I know the trauma was coming)	T+1
Write or draw what did happen:	Write or draw what did happen:	Write or draw what did happen:
What resource do you want here?	What resource do you want here?	What resource do you want here?
What response(s) needs to be completed:	What response(s) needs to be completed:	What response(s) needs to be completed:
T+2	T+3	T+4
Write or draw what did happen:	Write or draw what did happen:	Write or draw what did happen:
What resource do you want here?	What resource do you want here?	What resource do you want here?
What response(s) needs to be completed:	What response(s) needs to be completed:	What response(s) needs to be completed:

Restoring My Security

T+5 (Before I know the trauma was coming)	T+6	T+7 (Before I know the trauma was coming)
Write or draw what did happen:	**Write or draw what did happen:**	**Write or draw what did happen:**
What resource do you want here?	**What resource do you want here?**	**What resource do you want here?**
What response(s) needs to be completed:	**What response(s) needs to be completed:**	**What response(s) needs to be completed:**

1. Description of Trauma #7:

2. When did you know it was over?

3. What does it feel like in your body to know it is over?

4. Identify an image that represents that "it [this trauma] is over" to use in your trauma work:

5. Who do you want with you now in this trauma?

6. Work with your trauma, starting with T-7 (or T-5 if you want to break the trauma into fewer "slices"). Also, complete T+7 (or T+5 if you want to break the trauma into fewer "slices"). Work from T-7 to T+7, completing each block (what happened, resource you want there to help you through it, response that you need to complete regarding fight, flight, etc.). Use your holy imagination to see and feel each need being met.

Restoring My Security

T-7 (Before I know the trauma was coming)	T-6	T-5
Write or draw what did happen:	Write or draw what did happen:	Write or draw what did happen:
What resource do you want here?	What resource do you want here?	What resource do you want here?
What response(s) needs to be completed:	What response(s) needs to be completed:	What response(s) needs to be completed:
T-4	T-3	T-2
Write or draw what did happen:	Write or draw what did happen:	Write or draw what did happen:
What resource do you want here?	What resource do you want here?	What resource do you want here?
What response(s) needs to be completed:	What response(s) needs to be completed:	What response(s) needs to be completed:

T-1	T-0 (Before I know the trauma was coming)	T+1
Write or draw what did happen:	Write or draw what did happen:	Write or draw what did happen:
What resource do you want here?	What resource do you want here?	What resource do you want here?
What response(s) needs to be completed:	What response(s) needs to be completed:	What response(s) needs to be completed:
T+2	T+3	T+4
Write or draw what did happen:	Write or draw what did happen:	Write or draw what did happen:
What resource do you want here?	What resource do you want here?	What resource do you want here?
What response(s) needs to be completed:	What response(s) needs to be completed:	What response(s) needs to be completed:

T+5 (Before I know the trauma was coming)	T+6	T+7 (Before I know the trauma was coming)
Write or draw what did happen:	Write or draw what did happen:	Write or draw what did happen:
What resource do you want here?	What resource do you want here?	What resource do you want here?
What response(s) needs to be completed:	What response(s) needs to be completed:	What response(s) needs to be completed:

1. Description of Trauma #8:

2. When did you know it was over?

3. What does it feel like in your body to know it is over?

4. Identify an image that represents that "it [this trauma] is over" to use in your trauma work:

5. Who do you want with you now in this trauma?

6. Work with your trauma, starting with T-7 (or T-5 if you want to break the trauma into fewer "slices"). Also, complete T+7 (or T+5 if you want to break the trauma into fewer "slices"). Work from T-7 to T+7, completing each block (what happened, resource you want there to help you through it, response that you need to complete regarding fight, flight, etc.). Use your holy imagination to see and feel each need being met.

T-7 (Before I know the trauma was coming) Write or draw what did happen: What resource do you want here? What response(s) needs to be completed:	T-6 Write or draw what did happen: What resource do you want here? What response(s) needs to be completed:	T-5 Write or draw what did happen: What resource do you want here? What response(s) needs to be completed:
T-4 Write or draw what did happen: What resource do you want here? What response(s) needs to be completed:	T-3 Write or draw what did happen: What resource do you want here? What response(s) needs to be completed:	T-2 Write or draw what did happen: What resource do you want here? What response(s) needs to be completed:

T-1	T-0 (Before I know the trauma was coming)	T+1
Write or draw what did happen:	Write or draw what did happen:	Write or draw what did happen:
What resource do you want here?	What resource do you want here?	What resource do you want here?
What response(s) needs to be completed:	What response(s) needs to be completed:	What response(s) needs to be completed:
T+2	T+3	T+4
Write or draw what did happen:	Write or draw what did happen:	Write or draw what did happen:
What resource do you want here?	What resource do you want here?	What resource do you want here?
What response(s) needs to be completed:	What response(s) needs to be completed:	What response(s) needs to be completed:

Restoring My Security

T+5 (Before I know the trauma was coming)	T+6	T+7 (Before I know the trauma was coming)
Write or draw what did happen:	**Write or draw what did happen:**	**Write or draw what did happen:**
What resource do you want here?	**What resource do you want here?**	**What resource do you want here?**
What response(s) needs to be completed:	**What response(s) needs to be completed:**	**What response(s) needs to be completed:**

1. Description of Trauma #9:

2. When did you know it was over?

3. What does it feel like in your body to know it is over?

4. Identify an image that represents that "it [this trauma] is over" to use in your trauma work:

5. Who do you want with you now in this trauma?

6. Work with your trauma, starting with T-7 (or T-5 if you want to break the trauma into fewer "slices"). Also, complete T+7 (or T+5 if you want to break the trauma into fewer "slices"). Work from T-7 to T+7, completing each block (what happened, resource you want there to help you through it, response that you need to complete regarding fight, flight, etc.). Use your holy imagination to see and feel each need being met.

Restoring My Security

T-7 (Before I know the trauma was coming)	T-6	T-5
Write or draw what did happen:	Write or draw what did happen:	Write or draw what did happen:
What resource do you want here?	What resource do you want here?	What resource do you want here?
What response(s) needs to be completed:	What response(s) needs to be completed:	What response(s) needs to be completed:
T-4	T-3	T-2
Write or draw what did happen:	Write or draw what did happen:	Write or draw what did happen:
What resource do you want here?	What resource do you want here?	What resource do you want here?
What response(s) needs to be completed:	What response(s) needs to be completed:	What response(s) needs to be completed:

T-1	T-0 (Before I know the trauma was coming)	T+1
Write or draw what did happen:	Write or draw what did happen:	Write or draw what did happen:
What resource do you want here?	What resource do you want here?	What resource do you want here?
What response(s) needs to be completed:	What response(s) needs to be completed:	What response(s) needs to be completed:
T+2	T+3	T+4
Write or draw what did happen:	Write or draw what did happen:	Write or draw what did happen:
What resource do you want here?	What resource do you want here?	What resource do you want here?
What response(s) needs to be completed:	What response(s) needs to be completed:	What response(s) needs to be completed:

Restoring My Security

T+5 (Before I know the trauma was coming)	T+6	T+7 (Before I know the trauma was coming)
Write or draw what did happen:	**Write or draw what did happen:**	**Write or draw what did happen:**
What resource do you want here?	**What resource do you want here?**	**What resource do you want here?**
What response(s) needs to be completed:	**What response(s) needs to be completed:**	**What response(s) needs to be completed:**

1. Description of Trauma #10:

2. When did you know it was over?

3. What does it feel like in your body to know it is over?

4. Identify an image that represents that "it [this trauma] is over" to use in your trauma work:

5. Who do you want with you now in this trauma?

6. Work with your trauma, starting with T-7 (or T-5 if you want to break the trauma into fewer "slices"). Also, complete T+7 (or T+5 if you want to break the trauma into fewer "slices"). Work from T-7 to T+7, completing each block (what happened, resource you want there to help you through it, response that you need to complete regarding fight, flight, etc.). Use your holy imagination to see and feel each need being met.

T-7 (Before I know the trauma was coming)	**T-6**	**T-5**
Write or draw what did happen:	Write or draw what did happen:	Write or draw what did happen:
What resource do you want here?	What resource do you want here?	What resource do you want here?
What response(s) needs to be completed:	What response(s) needs to be completed:	What response(s) needs to be completed:
T-4	**T-3**	**T-2**
Write or draw what did happen:	Write or draw what did happen:	Write or draw what did happen:
What resource do you want here?	What resource do you want here?	What resource do you want here?
What response(s) needs to be completed:	What response(s) needs to be completed:	What response(s) needs to be completed:

T-1	T-0 (Before I know the trauma was coming)	T+1
Write or draw what did happen:	Write or draw what did happen:	Write or draw what did happen:
What resource do you want here?	What resource do you want here?	What resource do you want here?
What response(s) needs to be completed:	What response(s) needs to be completed:	What response(s) needs to be completed:
T+2	T+3	T+4
Write or draw what did happen:	Write or draw what did happen:	Write or draw what did happen:
What resource do you want here?	What resource do you want here?	What resource do you want here?
What response(s) needs to be completed:	What response(s) needs to be completed:	What response(s) needs to be completed:

Restoring My Security

T+5 (Before I know the trauma was coming)	T+6	T+7 (Before I know the trauma was coming)
Write or draw what did happen:	**Write or draw what did happen:**	**Write or draw what did happen:**
What resource do you want here?	**What resource do you want here?**	**What resource do you want here?**
What response(s) needs to be completed:	**What response(s) needs to be completed:**	**What response(s) needs to be completed:**

INDIVIDUAL HEARTWORK - STICKY MEMORIES

Write down the Sticky Memories that are unmoved or stuck after your Time Reversing Trauma™ work.

INDIVIDUAL HEARTWORK - OSCILLATION WITH JESUS™

We will be enjoying a tool called Oscillation with Jesus™. This is a powerful tool we use to process and resolve Traumas from Sticky Memories. It involves following an imaginal figure-eight with a positive and negative stimulus associated with the trauma. This technique helps us integrate new, positive emotional learning into the memory and reduce the emotional distress associated with it.

Begin by finding a comfortable position, either sitting or lying down. Take a deep breath in and slowly release it. Close your eyes and focus your attention on your breath, breathing in the life of God, exhaling stress.

Now, use your holy imagination to envision an invisible figure-eight in the air in front of you. Position it horizontally so that the loops are facing left and right. The right loop represents a safe- and belonging-filled memory with Jesus, while the left loop represents your Sticky Memory or Trauma Trigger.

As we start tracing the figure-eight, let's focus on the right loop, the safe memory with Jesus. Think about a highly positive image associated with this memory. It could be a place, a situation, or a feeling. Spend a few moments here, soaking in this positive sensation.

Now, as we trace the left loop, think about the trigger that you want to defuse. Be mindful of your emotions and stay within a manageable emotional zone, your Window of Tolerance. Spend less time on this side at the beginning, and slowly expand as the trigger loses its negative emotional valence.

Keep looping back and forth, spending more time on the positive side and gradually expanding your time on the negative side as negative emotions decrease. As you do this, observe how your body feels when exposed to both sides of the Oscillation.

Remember, Jesus is with you throughout this process. You are not alone. Keep breathing and tracing the figure-eight with your imagination, letting the Oscillation tool discharge and reconsolidate the Trigger.

When you are ready, take a deep breath in and slowly release it. Open your eyes and take a moment to ground yourself before resuming your study.

Use this QR code to access audible versions of activities.

INDIVIDUAL HEARTWORK – PAIN TO PURPOSE DRAWING™

Drawing One: Pain. For your first drawing, you will draw the felt sense of the Sticky Memory. In other words, if you could express the feeling you have within the memory through drawing, what would you draw? I am not asking you to draw the memory, but the feeling. Whatever comes to you is fine, just start drawing how you feel. In addition, remain in a non-judgmental attitude as you draw, as most of us are not artists. The important task is to draw your felt sense in the memory. After you work on Drawing One, check in with your body. What are you feeling? Honor these feelings.

Drawing Two: Opposite. For your second drawing, you will look at Drawing One and draw the opposite for Drawing Two. If you were to draw the opposite of the feeling of Drawing One, what would you draw? Ponder this, and draw whatever image comes to you. Remember, do not judge your drawing abilities. The important action is to draw the opposite of the first picture. After you work on

drawing two, check in with your body. What are you feeling? Honor these feelings. Ponder, how can I create more of these positive feelings?

Drawing Three: Kingdom Purpose. Next, we will use the Heart Journey™ Beautiful Place Prayer™. Ask the Lord, "What do You want to do with this pain to transform it into a Beautiful Place"? The Lord wants to take our wounded places, heal them, and use them for His purpose. Sit before Him and use Pneumaception™. Once He speaks to you, draw what He shows you. Notice the hope and Kingdom purpose in what He shows you. Allow hope to fill your heart as an anchor of your soul (Hebrews 6:19)

Memory #1: List the Trauma memory with which you will work.

Draw three drawings according to the directions above.

Drawing One: Pain

Drawing Two: Opposite

Drawing Three: Kingdom Purpose

Memory #2: List the Trauma memory with which you will work.

Draw three drawings according to the directions above.

Drawing One: Pain

Drawing Two: Opposite

Drawing Three: Kingdom Purpose

Memory #3: List the Trauma memory with which you will work.

Draw three drawings according to the directions above.

Drawing One: Pain

Drawing Two: Opposite

Drawing Three: Kingdom Purpose

Memory #4: List the Trauma memory with which you will work.

Draw three drawings according to the directions above.

Drawing One: Pain

Drawing Two: Opposite

Drawing Three: Kingdom Purpose

INDIVIDUAL HEARTWORK – BEAUTIFUL PLACE PRAYER™

Now list all your traumas below and pray the Beautiful Place Prayer™ over each one.

Trauma: _____

Write out your Beautiful Place Prayer™:

Trauma: _____

Write out your Beautiful Place Prayer™:

Trauma: _____

Write out your Beautiful Place Prayer™:

Trauma: _____

Write out your Beautiful Place Prayer™:

Trauma: _____

Write out your Beautiful Place Prayer™:

Trauma: _____

Write out your Beautiful Place Prayer™:

Trauma: _____

Write out your Beautiful Place Prayer™:

Trauma: _____

Write out your Beautiful Place Prayer™:

Trauma: _____

Write out your Beautiful Place Prayer™:

Trauma: _____

Write out your Beautiful Place Prayer™:

Trauma: _____

Write out your Beautiful Place Prayer™:

Trauma: _____

Write out your Beautiful Place Prayer™:

Trauma: _____

Write out your Beautiful Place Prayer™:

Trauma: _____

Write out your Beautiful Place Prayer™:

Trauma: _____

Write out your Beautiful Place Prayer™:

Trauma: _____

Write out your Beautiful Place Prayer™:

Trauma: _____

Write out your Beautiful Place Prayer™:

Trauma: _____

Write out your Beautiful Place Prayer™:

Trauma: _____

Write out your Beautiful Place Prayer™:

Trauma: _____

Write out your Beautiful Place Prayer™:

Trauma: _____

Write out your Beautiful Place Prayer™:

INDIVIDUAL HEARTWORK – FAMILY LINE

1. List the known sins and traumas from your family line (present and historical)

   a. Sins

   b. Traumas

2. Confess sins to the Lord and plead forgiveness and healing through the blood of Jesus over all sins and traumas. Write your confession below.

3. 1 John 3:8 (ESV) says, "The reason the Son of God appeared was to destroy the works of the devil." Pray with your Heart Group or your accountability partner to break the power of these sins and traumas over your family. Write your confession below.

INDIVIDUAL HEARTWORK- CHAPTER SEVEN REVIEW

Reflect on and journal your answers to the below questions. Your journal is a great, non-judgmental listener!

1. That was a difficult chapter. Be honest with yourself. How are you feeling right now? Relieved? Rattled?

2. Write down three ways you can glorify the Lord in this phase of your journey. Worship, perhaps?

3. Thus far, we have covered a lot of resources to help you regulate your nervous system. Were you able to recognize when you might need to bring resources in? If so, what were some of them?

4. How have you felt the presence of God with you this week while on the Heart Journey™?

5. If you had one thing to remember that Jesus pressed on your heart as you went through this lesson, what would it be?

HEART GROUP DISCUSSION – TIME TO SHARE.

1. Take time to share how you feel after Time Reversing Trauma™.

2. What was the hardest part for you? The easiest?

3. In moving forward from trauma, in what ways do you hope to keep Jesus engaged in your healing?

4. Did you find it helpful to explore sins and trauma from your genetic line and heritage? In what ways can you see they may have impacted you?

5. You have come a long way both individually and as a group. Discuss obstacles you have overcome and celebrate each other's success as a group.

Keystone Scriptures
for Restoring My Security

NOW MEMORIZE THESE KEYSTONE SCRIPTURES:

You've gone into my future to prepare the way,

and in kindness You follow behind me

to spare me from the harm of my past.

You have laid Your hand on me!

Psalm 139:5 (TPT)

The God of [ancient time] is a hiding place,

and underneath are the arms of eternity.

Deuteronomy 33:27 (LEB)

Because God is my refuge, the High God my very own home, evil can't get close to me,
harm can't get through the door. He ordered His angels to guard me wherever I go.

Psalm 91:9-11 (The Message)

LET US PRAY.

Heavenly Father,

We give You all our trauma, and we trust that You are turning every trauma into a blessing. You turn our ashes into beauty. It was one of Your first promises at the beginning of Your ministry, that You heal the brokenhearted and turn our ashes into beauty. We give You these ashes and pray that You would come into every area of our hearts and heal mightily. We pray that You would pull every bit of trauma out of places in our minds where it is stuck, that You would integrate into healthy spaces, and that You would soak Your Spirit into each place. Thank You that You Time Reversed™ all

our trauma! Lord, I thank You that my trauma is Time Reversed™ and that the enemy can no longer use trauma or the effects of it against me in Jesus' name. I speak that I am free from every impact of trauma.

Lord, regarding the sins of our forefathers, we ask that You forgive. We confess these things as sin (name each one out loud). I ask that You forgive my whole family line. Lord, I repent on behalf of my forefathers. (Name those things and ask the Lord to cover them). And Lord, we claim that Your blood covers every sin. We break the curse of where the enemy has been able to work through these family sins. We break the curse of all traumas that have been passed down. God, we break the genetic curse of traumas passed down before us (name the traumas.) Thank You that the enemy has no place in my family.

Now we move forward in that new freedom with nothing from the past holding us back. We believe we are free in Jesus' name based on Your finished work in the cross and resurrection. You have already transformed us so much on this beautiful, healing Heart Journey™. Thank You, Father.

Please continue Your good work, bringing us closer to You each day. May our hearts and minds continue to be open to Your renovations, and may we recognize where You are working in our lives. We pray that You would fill us with Your love, joy, and peace, and that we would continue to grow in our faith, hope, and trust in You. Lord, we pray for protection from the enemy, and that You would cover us with Your precious blood and shield us from harm.

We thank You, Lord, for Your grace and mercy, and for Your faithfulness to us. We give You all the praise, honor, and glory.

In Jesus' name, Amen.

Chapter

E I G H T

RESTORING MY BOUNDARIES

Let your Yes be simply Yes, and your No be simply No; anything more than that comes from the evil one.

Matthew 5:37 (AMPC)

INDIVIDUAL HEARTWORK – DAILY AND EXCESSIVE BURDENS

In the chart below, give examples of daily burdens that should be carried by individuals and excessive burdens that should be carried together.

Examples of Daily Load (baros)	Examples of Excessive Load (phortion)

After working on your chart, answer the following:

1. List any areas where you need to carry more of your own load.

2. List any areas where you need to allow others to carry their own load.

3. List any areas where you need to support others with an excessive load.

4. List any areas where you need to allow others to support you with an excessive load.

INDIVIDUAL HEARTWORK – TRUE AND FALSE SELF

1. Reflect below on when you show up as your "true self" vs. a "false self" in relationships.

2. What does it feel like to interact from your "true self"?

3. What does it feel like to interact from your "false self"?

4. Sit before Jesus and ask Him how He sees your "true self." Write below what He says to you.

INDIVIDUAL HEARTWORK – DEFINING MY BOUNDARIES

Clarify your personal boundaries by journaling on below areas of boundaries:

1. Values:

    a. What are your top ten values?

    b. Observe your life in the present season. Where do you live from these values?

    c. Where are you not living from your values?

    d. How can you more effectively use your choices to live within your values?

2. Words:

    a. How do you use words to reflect your values?

    b. How do you use words to reflect your "true self"?

    c. How can you more effectively use words to live within your true wants, needs, and values?

3. Actions and Behaviors:

    a. What behaviors do you engage with that feel like they come from your "true self"?

b. How do your actions reflect your boundaries?

c. How can you more effectively use your actions to live within your true wants, needs, and values?

4. Limits:

a. How does your use of limits reflect your "true self"?

b. How can you more effectively use limits to live within your true wants, needs, and values?

5. Choices:

    a. How do your choices around using time reflect your values and boundaries?

    b. How can you more effectively use your choices with time to live from your true wants, needs, and values?

6. Thoughts:

    a. What are your values for your thought life?

    b. How do your thoughts reflect your values?

c.   How can you more effectively use your thoughts to live within your true wants, needs, and values?

d.   How can you use your thoughts to think about yourself as God sees you?

7.   Attitudes:

a.   How would you describe your most prominent attitudes?

b.   How can you more effectively use your attitude to live within your values?

 **Heart** Journey

8. Personal Space:

a. When and where do you long for personal space?

b. How does your use of personal space reflect your "true self" needs?

c. How can you more effectively use personal space to live within your true wants, needs, and values?

9. Physical Distance:

a. When and why do you long for physical distance from others?

b. How does your use of physical distance reflect your "true self"?

c. How can you more effectively use physical distance or closeness to live within your true wants, needs, and values?

10. Stewarding of our Gifts/Talents:

a. What gifts and talents are yours to steward?

b. How does your use of gifts and talents reflect your values?

c. How can you more effectively use your gifts and talents to live within your values?

11. Stewarding of our Resources:

a. What resources has God given to you for stewarding?

b. What are your values about stewarding the resources God has given you?

c. How does your use of your resources reflect your "true self" boundaries?

d. How can you more effectively use your resources to live within your true wants, needs, and values?

12. Passions:

a. What passions has God given you to steward?

b. How can you more effectively express your passions from your "true self"?

13. Emotional Distance:

a. When and why do you need emotional distance?

b. How does your use of emotional distance reflect your true needs?

c. How can you more effectively use emotional distance and closeness to live within your true wants, needs, and values?

14. External Extensions of Me:

a. How do you use "extensions of me" (locks, fences, passwords, etc.) to set boundaries?

b. How can you more effectively use extensions of yourself (locks, fences, passwords, etc.) to live within your true wants, needs, and values?

INDIVIDUAL HEARTWORK – STEPPING OFF THE TRIANGLE OF PAIN

The three roles on the Triangle of Pain are persecutor, victim, and caretaker. Describe your interactions on the Triangle of Pain and how you have witnessed yourself engaging in each role.

Persecutor

Victim

Caretaker

What can you learn from this observation?

The three roles on the Triangle of Empowerment are coach, challenger, and creator. Describe how you can move off the Triangle of Pain and onto the Triangle of Empowerment in your relationships that experience duress.

INDIVIDUAL HEARTWORK – MATCHING MY INNER AND RELATIONAL LIFE

Notice the two sets of concentric circles below. For both sets of concentric circles, you will add the names of those in your life. Follow the steps below.

Step One. In the first set of concentric circles, you will write down names of those in your life regarding how close you "act" toward others. In other words, place everyone on the circle as your relationships looks from the outside as far as how close you and the person are. The farther into the center you place the name, the closer the relationship "appears," as far as amount of time and intimacy that you share with that person.

Step Two. In the second set of concentric circles, write down the names of those in your life. This time you will write down the names so that the distance from the center (the most intimate) reflects how your "true self" feels about each person. How much do you really trust each person? How safe do you really feel? It is critical that you are honest here about how close you truly feel to each person without judging yourself or them.

Step Three. Look for differences between the two circles.

Step Four. Write down what adjustments you will make to start graciously living out of your "true self".

Note: Occasionally, we are called to relate to those who are difficult for us.

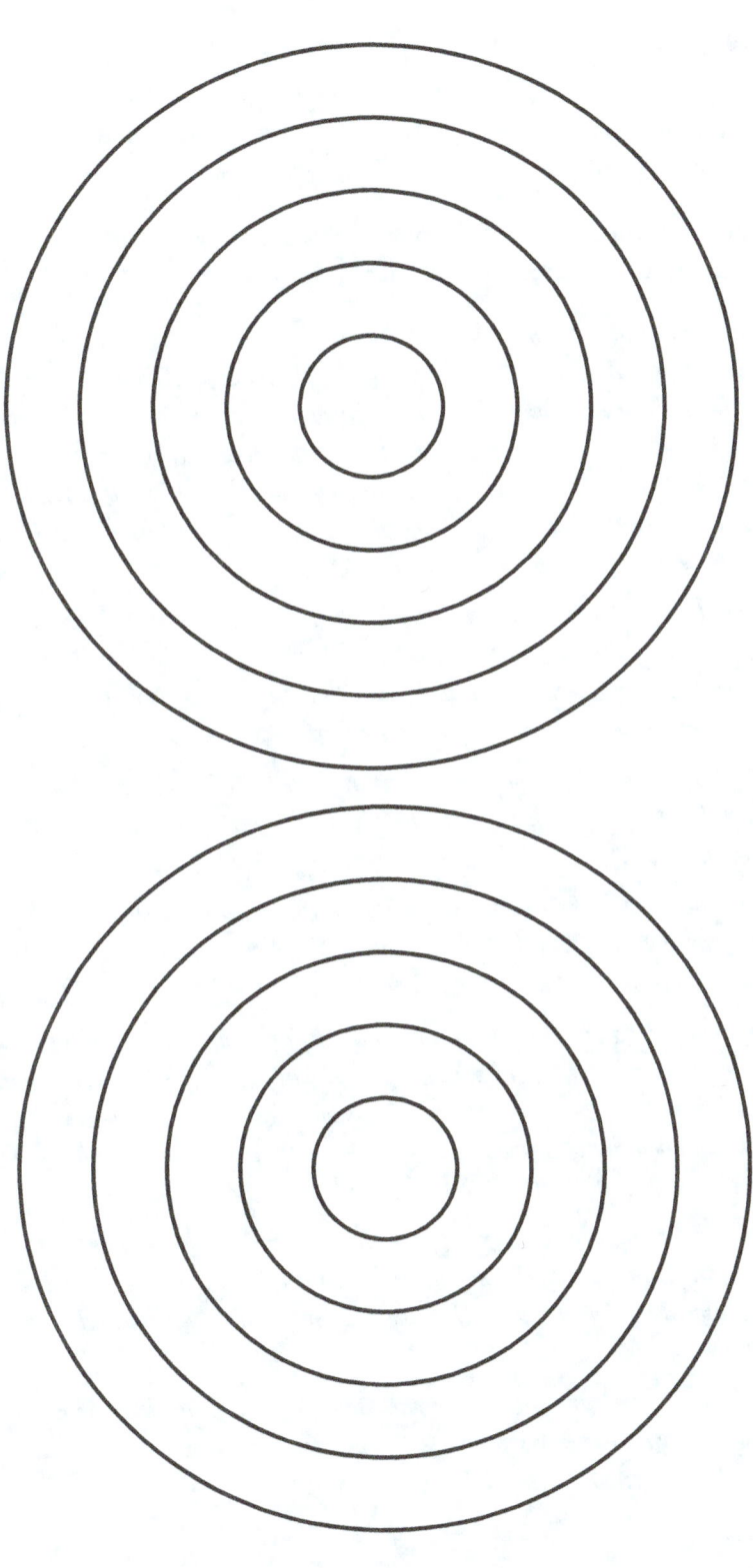

BOUNDARIES RESTORED ACTIVITY

Our next activity is a restorative boundary activity through which you will receive healing in your boundaries from the Lord as you use your holy imagination.

Relax into a comfortable chair, couch or bed, and use your holy imagination as Jesus gives you an experience of boundaries restored.

Beloved, take an instant to find a comfortable position and take a deep breath, inviting in the breath of God. As we begin this Boundaries Restored activity. Take a moment to remember instances where your needs, voice, and boundaries were not respected. Allow yourself to feel the pain associated with those experiences so we can open the Memory Reconsolidation Window for healing emotional learning. If that pain had a color or texture, what would it be? Remember that Jesus is with you as you bring these painful experiences to the surface.

Now, let's introduce a reparative Prediction Error to help restore your boundaries. Think about your personal space and what it would feel like to have it respected and acknowledged. Imagine Jesus providing you with experiences where your personal space is respected and acknowledged, both by himself and safe others.

What does it feel like to have your skin respected and only touched when you want to be touched, and how you want to be held? Imagine being hugged in a way that feels comfortable and safe.

What does it feel like to have your "no" respected, acknowledged, and responded to just the way you want it to be? What about your nonverbal "no"? What does it feel like to have that respected?

Now imagine having your need for space, distance, or time respected and heard. Imagine being listened to and responded to in a way that is just right for you. What does it feel like to have the space around your belongings respected? Imagine having your locked door and boundaries respected in just the right way. Allow yourself to feel a sense of safety and experience that "just right" feeling.

Think about areas in your life where what you have is not consistent with what you are longing for, yet you are struggling to ask. Imagine the Lord giving you strength to ask for what you need in a clearer way. Imagine receiving what you want and need. Imagine Jesus giving you a strong voice.

Think about clarifying your needs with someone significant in your life and them responding in a way that meets your needs just right. How does it feel to have someone respond and enjoy meeting your need in just the right way?

Restoring My Boundaries

We all needed healthy responses to our emotional necessities as young children. Maybe you did not have that as much as you needed. But right now, you can give yourself just the right amount of response. Imagine the Lord responding to your boundaries with love and respect. Imagine your ideal mom or dad responding just right to your boundaries. Feel that positive sense of being responded to, just right. Imagine Jesus giving you these experiences.

Now let's work on showing up with others in healthy ways. Imagine Jesus giving you wisdom and love to walk in healthy boundaries with others' wants and needs. What does it feel like when you respect someone else's personal space and meet their needs for space while still staying present with each other? Imagine Jesus helping you walk in this respect and sensitivity with wisdom.

What does it feel like to give someone else a safe, consensual hug while still holding onto yourself and Him?

Imagine responding to someone else's verbal or nonverbal "no" while still feeling completely loved. Jesus is with you.

What does it feel like to respect someone else's property by knocking on the door before entering? Can you feel the Lord's wholeness inside of you as you let others have their space while still meeting your own needs?

Allow yourself to feel a sense of peace and contentment as you continue to respect your own boundaries and those of others. Remember that Jesus is with you every step of the way, providing you with the wisdom and love to walk in healthy boundaries.

Now, let's imagine a scenario where you are present with Jesus, yourself, and others, and you are able to hold space for everyone while tuning most into Jesus. Take a moment to visualize this scenario. Imagine that you are in a group setting where there are other people around you. You are able to sense their presence, but you are also aware of your own personal space and boundaries. You are able to hold onto yourself and your connection with Jesus while also being present with others.

As you continue to visualize this scenario, imagine that Jesus is also present with you. You are able to feel His love and guidance as you navigate this social situation. You are able to tune into Him and His wisdom as you interact with others.

Notice how you are able to maintain your own boundaries and still be present with others. You are able to show respect for their personal space and needs while also holding onto your own. You are able to enjoy their company while also taking care of yourself.

As you continue to visualize this scenario, notice how you feel. Do you feel a sense of peace and contentment? Do you feel connected to Jesus and others in a healthy way? Allow yourself to fully experience these positive emotions.

Use this QR code to access audible versions of activities.

Now journal on your experience in the Boundaries Restored Activity.

INDIVIDUAL HEARTWORK – 360 QUADRANT EXERCISE

1. 360 Quadrant Exercise A

    a. Use a color-coded system to identify how safe each of the six quadrants in and around YOUR BODY feels. Feel into each quadrant and decode how safe each quadrant feels. "T" stands for on Top of you, "R" stands for your Right side, "L" stands for your Left side, "U" stands for Under you.

    b. Color "Safe" feeling quadrants green or write "Safe."

    c. Color "Mildly Unsafe" feeling quadrants yellow or write "MUS."

    d. Color "Unsafe" feeling quadrants orange or write "US."

    e. Color "Very Unsafe" feeling quadrants red or write "VUS."

    f. Color "Numb" feeling quadrants blue or write "Unsafe."

    g. If you have a new hurtful memory that comes up, write it down and rework it using the steps for Satisfy Unmet Needs™ or Time Reverse Traumas™.

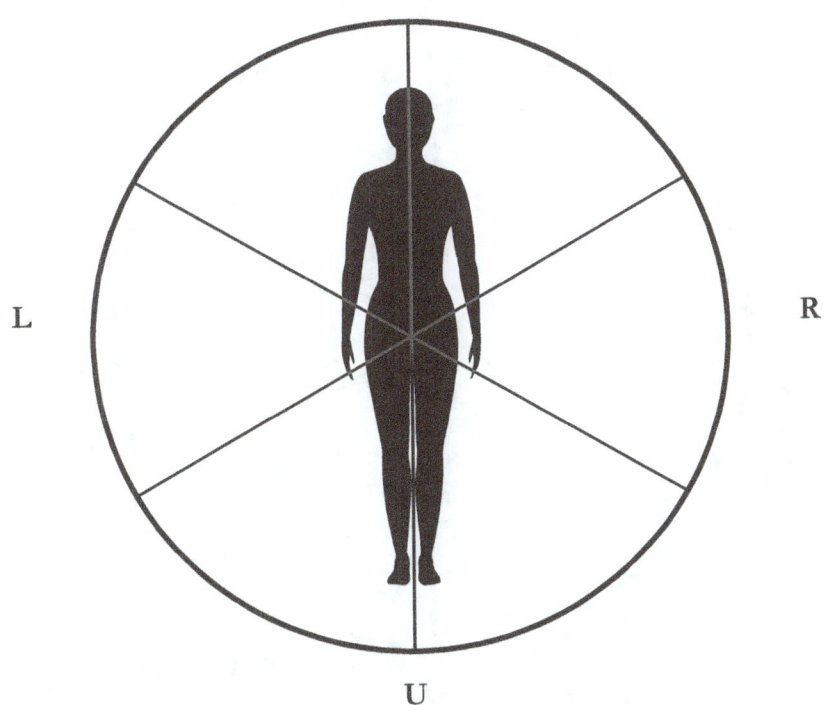

2. 360 Quadrant Exercise B

    a. Use a color-coded system to identify how safe each of the six quadrants in and around YOUR BODY feels. Feel into each quadrant and decode how safe each quadrant feels. "T" stands for on Top of you, "F" stands for your Front side, "B" stands for your Backside, "U" stands for Under you.

    b. Color "Safe" feeling quadrants green or write "Safe."

    c. Color "Mildly Unsafe" feeling quadrants yellow or write "MUS."

    d. Color "Unsafe" feeling quadrants orange or write "US."

    e. Color "Very Unsafe" feeling quadrants red or write "VUS."

    f. Color "Numb" feeling quadrants blue or write "Unsafe."

    g. If you have a new hurtful memory that comes up, write it down and rework it using the steps for Satisfy Unmet Needs™ or Time Reverse Traumas™.

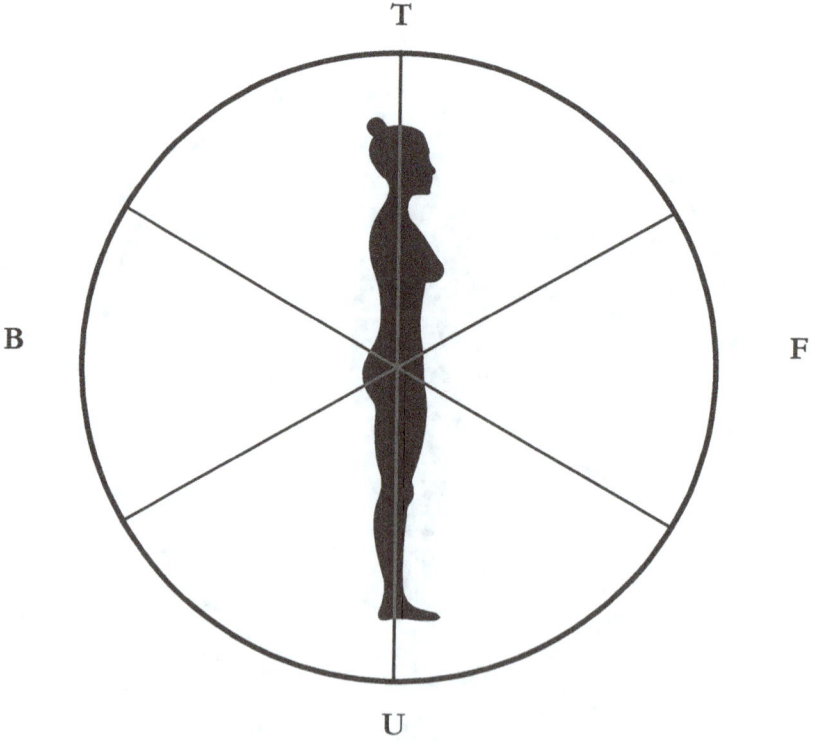

3. 360 Quadrant Exercise C

   a. Use a color-coded system to identify how safe each of the six quadrants in and around YOUR BODY feels. Feel into each. "F" stands for your Front side, "B" stands for your Backside, "U" stands for Under you, "T" stands for Top.

   b. Color "Safe" feeling quadrants green or write "Safe."

   c. Color "Mildly Unsafe" feeling quadrants yellow or write "MUS."

   d. Color "Unsafe" feeling quadrants orange or write "US."

   e. Color "Very Unsafe" feeling quadrants red or write "VUS."

   f. Color "Numb" feeling quadrants blue or write "Unsafe."

   g. If you have a new hurtful memory that comes up, write it down and rework it using the steps for Satisfy Unmet Needs™ or Time Reverse Traumas™.

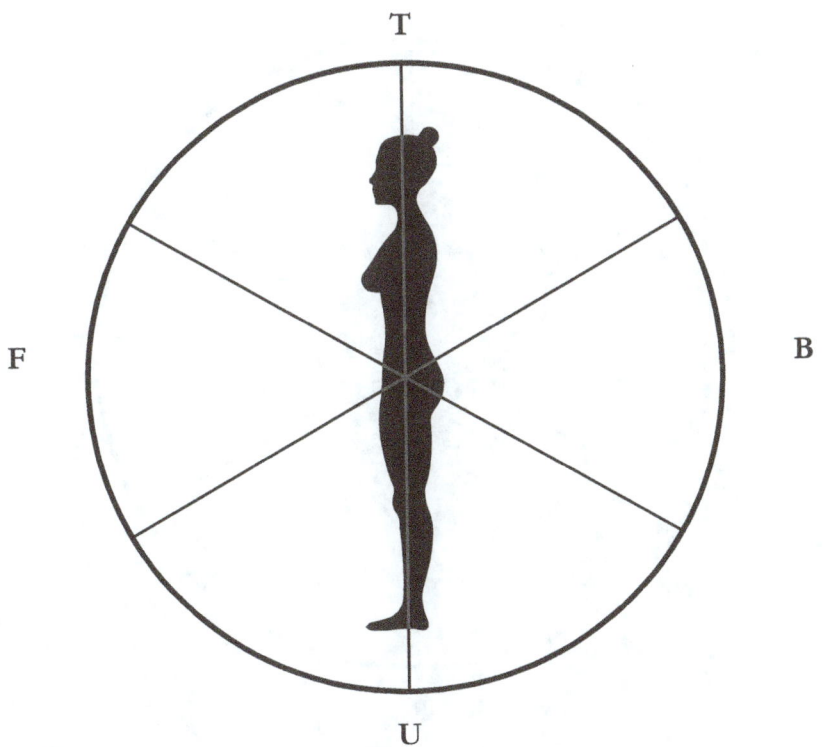

4.   360 Quadrant Exercise D

a.   Use a color-coded system to identify how safe each of the six quadrants in and around YOUR BODY feels. Feel into each quadrant and decode how safe each quadrant feels. "L" stands for your Left side, "F" stands for your Front side, "B" stands for your Backside, "R" stands for your Right side.

b.   Color "Safe" feeling quadrants green or write "Safe."

c.   Color "Mildly Unsafe" feeling quadrants yellow or write "MUS."

d.   Color "Unsafe" feeling quadrants orange or write "US."

e.   Color "Very Unsafe" feeling quadrants red or write "VUS."

f.   Color "Numb" feeling quadrants blue or write "Unsafe."

g.   If you have a new painful memory arise, write it down and rework it using the steps for unmet needs or traumas.

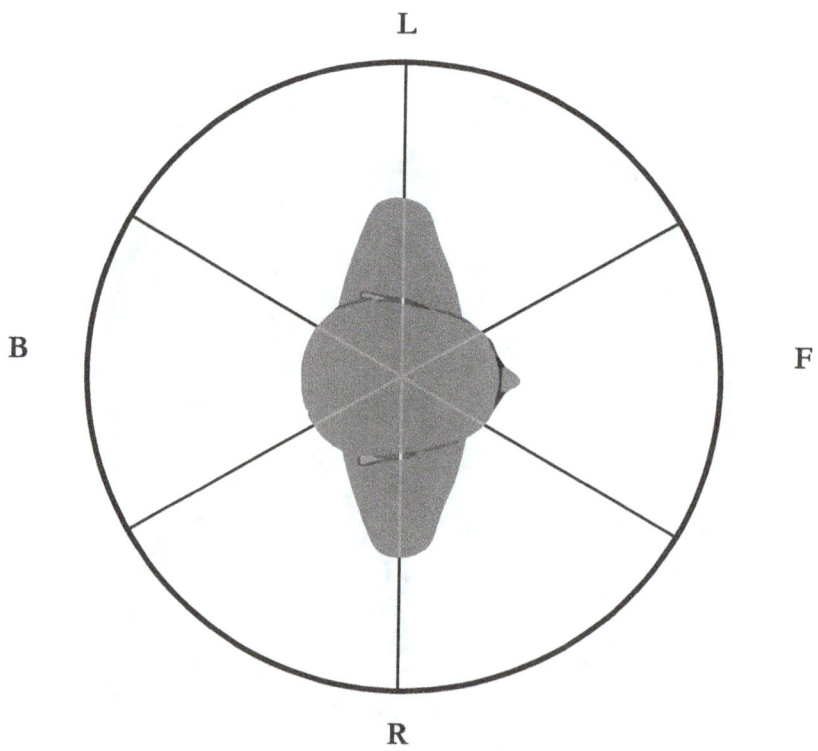

5. Now list all areas in which you felt distress.

6. Next, take a moment to use your holy imagination to imagine the love of God going into every area of your body where you have implicit somatic distress.

360 QUADRANT PRAYER ACTIVITY

Let us take a moment to use our holy imagination to envision the love of Jesus entering every area of our body where we may have experienced somatic distress. Let us close our eyes and take a deep breath, allowing ourselves to fully surrender to His presence.

As we breathe in, let us envision the love of Jesus filling every area in our body with His light, warmth, and healing. Let us allow His love to permeate every cell in our body. Now welcome Him to be present with your body.

Now let us focus on specific areas of our body that may be carrying somatic distress. Perhaps it is our chest, where we hold our heart and our emotions. Let us visualize Jesus' love entering our chest, warming and soothing any pain that we may be carrying in our hearts.

Or perhaps it is our stomach, where we may feel anxiety or tension. Let us envision Jesus' love entering our stomach, relaxing our muscles and calming our nerves.

As we continue to breathe deeply and visualize Jesus' love entering every area of our body, let us feel a sense of peace and comfort wash over us. Let us know that we are not alone, and that Jesus is with us, bringing healing and restoration to every part of our being.

Name each area that felt activated and welcome Him in. Take time with this, softening into His presence providing safety to each body memory.

Let us take another deep breath, breathing in His presence, and as we exhale, release any remaining tension or fear. Let us know that we are loved, we are cherished, and we are held in the loving arms of Jesus. Amen.

Use this QR code to access audible versions of activities.

INDIVIDUAL HEARTWORK – FREEDOM FROM FALSE GUILT

Go through this activity and then journal on the prompts afterwards.

FREEDOM FROM FALSE GUILT ACTIVITY

Take a moment to get comfortable as you prepare to use your holy imagination. Imagine a Saturday afternoon where you have two hours to do whatever you want to do. During these two hours, you are absolutely forbidden to have any guilt whatsoever. Imagine that your ability to use guilt against yourself is erased.

What would it be like to have two hours to live without that false sense of guilt? We are talking about that guilt that has no basis in reality, that false sense of "I should be doing something more." All of the "shoulds" have been lifted off you. What would you do with two hours without any guilt or "shoulds"? Really think about this, Beloved. What would you do?

No responsibilities, no guilt, no "shoulds." Just allow yourself to imagine what that would be like. Jesus is giving you this freedom from false guilt and shame as a gift. Now, what would you do with the whole day without guilt and "shoulds," maybe even adding in some of your responsibilities without all the false guilt and "shoulds."

Now expanding on our activity, what would your life be like without false guilt and "shoulds" for a whole week? Imagine how your life might be different, just imagine it. Jesus wants this for you. Allow yourself to soften into the freedom.

When you go to the movies, you suspend your disbelief. In the same way as in a movie, imagine what it would be like to let go of all the false guilt and feelings of not being good enough. What would your life be like if your whole life were like that, my friend? This is what God wants for you.

The life He wants for you is one of freedom where you are a cheerful giver, not giving or doing out of compulsion. God never gives out of guilt. He never does what He does out of guilt, but only out of purpose and love. He created you to live out of purpose, to laugh, to have good boundaries, to be able to know who you are, and to love who you are as well as to be able to be with others while still being you. Now ask Him, "Lord, help me set boundaries with myself so that I do not allow false guilt."

Use this QR code to access audible versions of activities.

Journal on your experience.

1. How easy or difficult was it for you to imagine yourself free from false guilt?

2. What changes will you commit to regarding setting boundaries on false guilt in your thought life?

INDIVIDUAL HEARTWORK – CHAPTER EIGHT REVIEW

Reflect on and journal your answers to the below questions.

1. What it is like to have your boundaries crossed?

2. When in this exercise, did you begin to realize the importance of boundaries?

3. How did it feel to work through the exercises and learn how to establish healthy boundaries?

4. What rooms of your heart home, or areas of your life, do you feel are benefitting the most from reestablished, healthy boundaries?

5. Think of at least three way you can invite Jesus into these rooms when healthy boundaries may begin to cave. Share this with your accountability or prayer partner for support.

6.   What did you discover about your body and boundaries?

HEART GROUP DISCUSSION - TIME TO SHARE.

1.   As you prayed and went through this lesson, which Scripture did God reveal to you to support you in this phase of the journey? Share with your group or safe person why this particular Scripture resonates with you and how you plan to integrate it into your healing.

2.   How did you feel at the beginning of this lesson before allowing the Lord to work with your unhealthy boundaries?

3.   How do you feel now after inviting the Lord into those ruptured boundaries and musty parts of your heart home?

4. As you continue on this Heart Journey™, share with your group and/or prayer and accountability partner how you intend to address when healthy boundaries begin to cave. What is your maintenance plan for this room in your heart home?

5. This chapter likely brought out even more painful memories and trauma caused by boundary ruptures and interacting from within the Triangle of Pain. Be authentic with your small group sisters and/or prayer and accountability partner. Share how they can help support you in this phase of your Heart Journey™.

Keystone Scriptures for Restoring Boundary Ruptures

NOW MEMORIZE THESE KEYSTONE SCRIPTURES:

The boundary lines have fallen for me in pleasant places; surely I have a delightful inheritance.

Psalm 16:6 (NIV)

God will never be mocked! For what you plant will always be the very thing you harvest. The harvest you reap reveals the seed that you planted. If you plant the corrupt seeds of self-life into this natural realm, you can expect a harvest of corruption. If you plant the good seeds of Spirit-life you will reap beautiful fruits that grow from the everlasting life of the Spirit.

Galatians 6:7-8 (TPT)

Never move a long-standing boundary line.

Proverbs 23:10a (TPT)

Every believer is ultimately responsible for his or her own conscience.

Galatians 6:5 (TPT)

LET US PRAY.

Heavenly Father,

Thank You for being with us as we continue on this journey. Working on boundaries challenged us all on so many levels. Help each of us to reestablish healthy boundaries and keep them maintained. And we know that we can only do so by Your strength.

Also, Father, thank You for teaching us about the Triangle of Pain. Help us to keep our spiritual eyes open to it and the different enemy attacks that may try to lure us back onto it. Help us to stay strong and to stay off it. Thank You, Father, for continuing to heal these parts of our heart home.

In Jesus' name, Amen.

Chapter

NINE

RESTORING MY PEACE

Then Jesus said to the woman at His feet, "All your sins are forgiven."

Luke 7:48 (TPT)

SUPPLIES

As you engage with your Chapter Six Heartwork you will need the following materials: your *Heart Journey™ Journal*, your Chapter Five timeline work, a pen or pencil, and pictures of yourself through time covering early childhood, adolescence, and adulthood at various stages. If possible, use pictures from time periods when you may have liked yourself less. (e.g., in her adolescence Deborah struggled with eating disorders, so her weight would go up and down, where she would be very thin, then bigger, so she used pictures where she was unhappy with her body for the exercise ahead.) We want to get at the heart of your self-resentment.

IDENTIFY RESENTMENTS

Look over your timeline in your *Heart Journey™ Journal* work from Chapter Five, and list each person below that was involved in you experiencing traumas and unmet needs.

1.	16.
2.	17.
3.	18.
4.	19.
5.	20.
6.	21.
7.	22.
8.	23.
9.	24.
10.	25.
11.	26.
12.	27.
13.	28.
14.	29.
15.	30.

Now sit before the Lord. Ask Him to search your heart for anyone else for whom you might have resentments. Add the names He shows you below. Also add "God" and "life in general" as well.

1.	5.
2.	6.
3.	7.
4.	8.

INDIVIDUAL HEARTWORK – UNBURDENING FROM RESENTMENT™: OTHERS

You will work through your list of resentments above, one at a time, including resentments toward others, God, and even life in general. You will work on a chart that has four columns, namely, "The Person I Resent," "Why I Resent That Person," "What is Threatened?" and "My Part." It will be important to determine what is threatened (physiological needs, safety, love & belonging, esteem, etc.) in the process. This will help you understand why you are angry. Then, in the "My Part" section, you will list any culpability you might have in the situation. This will require humility. At times, you have no part in the actual trauma or unmet need, but as time has passed, your part might be continuing to believe a lie about yourself, harboring resentment, or re-enacting traumas by choosing unhelpful relationships. Look for where you are participating with the enemy's destruction in "My Part."

You will go through the same process with each person on your list, including "God" and "life in general." Start with column one, and the person you resent the most. In column one, "People I Resent," write the person's name. In column two, write down all the person did that hurt or offended you.

In column three, you will identify what was threatened in the situation that caused the resentment. Using a Christian perspective on Maslow's Hierarchy of Needs, consider the following needs that may be threatened when we feel resentment:

1. Physiological needs (such as food, water, and shelter)

2. Safety needs (such as protection from harm or danger)

3. Love and belonging needs (such as connection and intimacy with others)

4. Value needs (such as respect and being valued for who we are)

5. Purpose fulfillment (such as spiritual growth and achieving one's full potential in Christ)

As you work through each resentment, ask yourself if your physiological needs, sense of safety, love and belonging, sense of value, or purpose fulfillment were threatened. Did the situation threaten your need for sleep, food, or survival? Did someone violate your safety or cause harm to you? Did someone hurt your sense of love and belonging? Did you feel undervalued or disrespected? Did the situation keep you from achieving your full potential in Christ? Record what was threatened in column three.

In column four, take the time to reflect on your part in the resentment. Are there any fears or selfish behaviors that you are holding onto that are contributing to the resentment? Are you perpetuating cycles that others began, such as continuing to reject yourself long after the situation has ended? Consider if there are any underlying insecurities or fears, such as a fear of rejection or abandonment, or a lack of trust in others, that you need to acknowledge as your part in the resentment. It is important to take responsibility for our own actions and attitudes in order to heal and move forward.

As you work through this activity, it is important to be honest with yourself and include any resentments you may hold toward God. Do not ignore or dismiss these feelings, as they can be a significant barrier to healing and moving forward. We must be rigorously honest. God knows it all anyway! Deborah, herself discovered that she had been angry with God for years without even realizing it. Take your time to reflect on your attitude toward life as well. Are there any negative beliefs or resentments you hold toward life in general that may be holding you back? Remember, this activity is about taking inventory of all the issues that may be preventing you from living a fulfilling life and working toward resolving them. We are wholeheartedly cleaning the inside of the cup (Matthew 23:25-26).

The Person I Resent	Why I Resent That Person	What is Threatened? (physiological needs, safety, love & belonging, value, purpose)	My Part

The Person I Resent	Why I Resent That Person	What is Threatened? (physiological needs, safety, love & belonging, value, purpose)	My Part

The Person I Resent	Why I Resent That Person	What is Threatened? (physiological needs, safety, love & belonging, value, purpose)	My Part

After you have completed your chart, follow the following steps:

1. Go through your part and out loud, give it to the Lord, saying, "I forgive myself for each thing that is my part. I forgive myself, and I ask for Your forgiveness, Lord. I receive Your forgiveness for each one of those things." This helps you forgive yourself and receive God's forgiveness for each item.

2. Ask God to move in that area. Where you have fears, for example, give those to the Lord and make a choice to trust Him in a deeper way.

3. Ask Him to help you trust Him.

ACTIVATION PRAYER

Lord, we give You each area where we have a part, whether it be fear of rejection, selfishness, fear of trusting, food insecurity, or money insecurity. We choose to trust You, and we ask that You cleanse us of every place where we have unrighteousness, and that You would make us whole in these areas. We pray for each area we have identified, confessing our sins, fears, and lack of faith. We pray that You would transform and change us. Thank You for forgiving us. Thank You that by Your wounds we are healed and that we are forgiven because of the punishment that was put on You.

In Jesus' name, Amen.

Beloved, now receive that forgiveness.

Next you will verbally forgive and release each person on your list by forgiving them based on all Jesus did for you and all of us. Here are the steps for verbally forgiving and releasing each person on your list:

1. Take a deep breath and focus your mind on Jesus and His sacrifice for you on the cross.

2. Begin by reading the name of the first person on your "The Person I Resent" list and say out loud, "I forgive [person's name] for [specific offense]."

3. Remember that when Jesus died on the cross, He took on all of our sins, including the sins of the person you are forgiving. Thank Jesus for this gift of forgiveness and ask Him to help you forgive the person completely.

4. Say out loud, "I release [person's name] from the debt I held against them. I choose to let go of all resentment and bitterness toward them."

5. Repeat this process for each person on your list, taking your time with each one. Remember that forgiveness is a process, and it may take time and effort to fully forgive and release each person.

6. After you have forgiven and released each person, thank Jesus for His forgiveness and grace in your life. Ask Him to continue to help you walk in forgiveness and healing.

ACTIVATION PRAYER

Dear Jesus, as I read through my list of resentments, I choose to forgive each person based on all that You have done for me and all of us. I know that when You died on the cross, You took on all of our sins, including the sins of those who have hurt me. Thank You, Lord, for dying for me. I choose to release each person from the debt I held against them and to let go of all resentment and bitterness toward them. Please help me to fully forgive and release each person, and to walk in healing and freedom. Thank You for Your forgiveness and grace in my life. In Your name I pray, Amen.

It is also important to acknowledge and address any resentments you may hold toward God and life in general. If you are struggling with resentment toward God, take the time to sit down and have an honest conversation with Him. Admit your feelings and ask for forgiveness for holding those negative emotions against Him. Ask Him to show you how He sees the situation. Surrender those feelings to Him and trust that He has a plan for you, even if you do not understand it. Similarly, if you are resentful toward life in general, take a moment to reflect on your attitude toward life before the Lord and ask for the strength to change it. Ask Jesus to help you see things from His point of view and write down what He shows you below.

Lastly, I encourage you to share your Unburden form Resentment™: Others work with a trusted friend, whether a small group sister or your prayer/accountability partner. When we confess our sins one to another, we are healed, and it can help you with a commitment to forgive (James 5:16).

INDIVIDUAL HEARTWORK – UNBURDENING FROM RESENTMENT™: SELF AT EVERY AGE

Complete the chart below. Be sure to address all three domains in your resentments toward yourself at each age range: who you are (your personality), what you did (your choices), and your physical appearance. For the "How God Sees Me" section, sit before the Lord and ask Him how He sees you at that age and stage. In the "Self-Momming™" column, write to that part of you as from your ideal mothering part of self.

My Age	Why I Resent Myself	How God Sees Me	Self-Momming™
Myself 0-5			
Myself 6-10			

Myself 11-14			
Myself 15-18			
Myself 18-current			

FORGIVING MYSELF ACTIVITY

To begin this activity, get comfortable and breathe in the Ruach breath of God. I wonder if you can think back to yourself early in life. You can open your eyes or close them, Beloved. Imagine Jesus with you, in you, filling you, giving you strength and grace to love and forgive yourself.

Imagine yourself as a newborn baby, then a toddler. Consider if there is anything you are holding against that precious little one. If so, speak out loud, "I choose to forgive myself. I choose to forgive you and love you as a baby and a toddler." Now, imagine hugging yourself and loving that part of you with Jesus supporting you.

And now, as a preschooler, what were you like? Can you get that image in your mind? Is there something you hold against this little one? It is time to stop holding anything against that little one because she was not at fault—at all. Share your love with that precious preschooler with Jesus supporting you.

Next imagine yourself in elementary school, thinking of yourself in kindergarten, then in first grade. What were you like in second grade, third grade, fourth grade, and fifth grade? Is there anything you are holding against that little one? If so, it is time to let it go and to let that little one experience the freedom of having nothing held against her. Allow her to receive your love and God's love.

Now we go to middle school. Is there something you have been holding against yourself for when you were in sixth, seventh, or eighth grade? Maybe you felt awkward and judged yourself. It is time to let that go. Let that part of you love, be loved, and receive love with Jesus supporting you.

What about that ninth, tenth, eleventh, or twelfth grade self and the mistakes that precious one made? Can you forgive her? When you forgive, you are agreeing and becoming one with the Lord and His Word. Choose to love that one at every awkward stage and brilliant moment as well. Just love that precious one, letting go of any resentments.

And now, what about that young adult, ages eighteen, nineteen, twenty, and twenty-one? It is important to forgive that young one for anything you are holding against her. Love and embrace her, giving her that mothering that she needs.

What about that older twenty-one year-old self? And all the way up through to whatever age you are. Think about yourself in your twenties. Love that twenty-something year old. Forgive her for any mistakes she made, embracing her fully, holding nothing against her, and receiving the Lord's love and forgiveness.

And now you are in your thirties. If not, look ahead and forgive that thirty year old for anything that might be there that you might be holding against her. She did the best she could.

For that forty year old, love her, too. If you are not forty, look ahead and love that forty-year-old woman, forgiving her for any mistakes she made or will make.

Do the same for that fifty-year-old woman, and the woman in her sixties, seventies, eighties, and beyond. Love her, accept her, and forgive her, receiving God's love for her and forgiveness for her.

Now, bring all those parts of you to Jesus, receive the love of the Father and the love of your Self-mom. Take some time to reflect on this as you feel God's love, your own love for yourself, and the freedom you now have.

Use this QR code to access audible versions of activities.

Lord, You're so kind and tenderhearted and so patient with people who fail You!

Your love is like a flooding river overflowing its banks with kindness.

Psalm103:8 (TPT)

INDIVIDUAL HEARTWORK – MAKING AMENDS

To begin, examine your resentment list, specifically the "My Part" column from your Individual Heartwork - Unburdening from Resentment™: Others. Consider the individuals to whom you need to make amends, including yourself and list them on the chart below. Then begin to pray over and write down what form your amends should take. Making amends can take various forms, such as repaying what is owed, changing our behavior, or offering apologies.

Avoid rushing into immediate apologies and instead let the Spirit guide you toward genuine amends, free from fear or guilt. Be cautious not to over-apologize or under-apologize, respecting healthy boundaries. Consider meaningful ways to apologize or make amends, such as writing letters or notes, making restitution for past wrongs, praying for those you have hurt, or engaging in acts of service. You might also consider a meaningful act in their honor. For example, if you bullied someone with Down Syndrome in high school or middle school, you could make a donation to the Down Syndrome Foundation. The most significant way to make amends is through lasting behavioral change.

Seek support from your small group sisters, accountability/prayer partner, or trusted individuals, as this process is not meant to be undertaken alone.

Additionally, remember to extend forgiveness and make amends to yourself. Treat yourself with the same kindness and compassion you would offer a dear friend.

Trust in God's timing for each situation, checking off completed amends along the way. Remember that this process may not happen overnight, and it may take years as it unfolds according to God's perfect timing.

Name of Person w/Whom to Make Amends	How I will Make Amends	Date Completed

INDIVIDUAL HEARTWORK – STICKY RESENTMENTS

Now we will work with your Sticky Resentments. Use the chart below.

1. Make a list of those with whom you have a Sticky Resentment in column one.

2. List the ten blessings you want most in your own life in column two.

3. Make a copy of this chart and post the list and the blessings where you will see it often.

4. Wholeheartedly pray the list of blessings for those with whom you have Sticky Resentments at least two times daily.

5. Watch your resentments ease as God's love fills you.

People with whom I harbor Sticky Resentments	Ten Blessings I Want Most in My Life

INDIVIDUAL HEARTWORK – CHAPTER NINE REVIEW

Reflect on and journal your answers to the below questions.

1. What was the hardest part of the exercises in this chapter? Why was that the case?

2. Do you feel completely free from resentment and unforgiveness or do you need to do more work in this area?

3. How has your mind changed at this phase of the journey?

4. How has you heart changed at this point?

5. What rooms of your heart home do you feel are benefitting the most from unforgiveness and breaking free from resentment?

6. Think of at least three ways you can invite Jesus into these rooms when resentments creep back in. Share this with your accountability or prayer partner for support.

HEART GROUP DISCUSSION – TIME TO SHARE.

1. As you went through this lesson, think of one thing of significance that God revealed to you to support you in this phase of the journey. Share with your group or a safe person.

2. How did you feel at the beginning of this lesson before breaking free from resentment and unforgiveness?

3. How do you feel now after inviting the Lord in and praying over those resentments and unforgiveness?

4. As you continue on this Heart Journey™, share with your group and/or prayer and accountability partner how you intend to address when resentments and un-forgiveness begin to creep back in. What is your maintenance plan for this room in your heart home?

5. This chapter likely brought out even more painful memories caused by resentment and un-forgiveness. Be authentic with your small group sisters and/or prayer and accountability partner. Share how they can help support you in this phase of your Heart Journey™.

LET US PRAY.

Heavenly Father,

I am beginning to feel so free … free from resentments, unforgiveness, and so many issues that have weighed heavy on my heart for far too long. Thank You for being with us as we continue on this journey. Please continue to show us areas that may still need renovation. We want to heal fully, and know that can only happen through Your loving guidance. Thank You, Father, for continuing to heal these parts of our heart home.

In Jesus' name, Amen.

Keystone Scriptures for Restoring My Peace

NOW MEMORIZE THESE KEYSTONE SCRIPTURES:

And become useful and helpful and kind to one another, tenderhearted (compassionate, understanding, loving-hearted), forgiving one another [readily and freely], as God in Christ forgave you.

Ephesians 4:32 (AMPC)

Though the mountains be shaken and the hills be removed, yet My unfailing love for you will not be shaken nor My covenant of peace be removed," says the Lord, who has compassion on you.

Isaiah 54:10 (NIV)

With my whole heart, with my whole life, and with my innermost being, I bow in wonder and love before You, the holy God! Yahweh, You are my soul's celebration. How could I ever forget the miracles of kindness You've done for me? You kissed My heart with forgiveness, in spite of all I've done. You've healed me inside and out from every disease. You've rescued me from hell and saved my life. You've crowned me with love and mercy. You satisfy my every desire with good things.

You've supercharged my life so that I soar again like a flying eagle in the sky!

You're a God who makes things right, giving justice to the defenseless.

Psalm 103: 1-6 (TPT)

Chapter

T E N

RESTORING MY LOST OPPORTUNITIES

Therefore, if anyone is in Christ, the new creation has come: The old has gone, the new is here!

2 Corinthians 5:17 (NIV)

SUPPLIES

For this chapter's Heartwork, you will need a pen or pencil, colored markers or pencils and your *Heart Journey*™ *Journal.*

INDIVIDUAL HEARTWORK - CEDE TO ACCEPTANCE

Journal your answers to these questions:

1. Where do you need to cede to the kind of acceptance you learned about in your Heart Journey(TM) book?

2. What can you change?

3. What is not yours to change?

4. Ask the Lord, "Where am I in a needless power struggle?"

5. How can you cede to acceptance to remove yourself from the power struggle?

INDIVIDUAL HEARTWORK – CEDE TO GRATITUDE

1. Journal below on the resources that got you through your traumas and losses. Then write a statement of gratitude for those resources.

2. Write down at least five resources on the inside of you that are characteristics that helped you through (e.g., resilience, determination, resourcefulness, compassion, creativity, etc.). Then write a statement of gratitude. Relish and be grateful for those things that helped you get through. Those things have become assets in your life and personality.

3. Take a moment to reflect on the abundance of people, places, and things you are grateful for in your life. Create a gratitude list comprising twenty things, people, or situations that you genuinely appreciate. Allow yourself to dive deep and explore the aspects, big and small, that bring gratitude into your life. As you jot down each item, be mindful of how gratitude has the power to uplift you, as the Lord intended. "And let the peace of Christ rule in your hearts, to which indeed you were called in one body. And be thankful" (Colossians 3:15 ESV).

As you journal below, notice how your body and emotions respond as you delve into this exercise. What sensations are you experiencing? How does it feel to cultivate gratitude? Now, observe the shifts in your body and emotions, recognizing the transformative nature of practicing gratitude. Take your time with this exercise, savoring the process of acknowledging and embracing the blessings that surround you. Allow gratitude to wash over you, filling your journal and your heart with an overwhelming sense of appreciation and joy.

4. Journal on your "Cede to Gratitude Action Plan," i.e., write your plan for incorporating gratitude more into your life as a habit.

   My Cede to Gratitude Action Plan is:

INDIVIDUAL HEARTWORK – CEDE TO SPIRITUAL DISCIPLINE

Below, write down the Spiritual Disciplines in which you are desiring to grow. Write down your plan for growing in Spiritual Disciplines (e.g., prayer, Bible reading, waiting on the Lord/stillness and listening to Him, worship, etc.). Be sure to seek the Lord on where He wants you to grow. Pay close attention to the specific areas the Holy Spirit is highlighting, where He desires to see you flourish and experience transformation. Just as Mary found immeasurable value at the feet of Jesus, may you, too, find deep fulfillment and a profound sense of purpose as you pray, listen, wait upon, and worship our Lord.

1. I will incorporate more prayer into my daily life by:

2. I will incorporate more Scripture into my daily life by:

3. I will incorporate more waiting on the Lord into my daily life by:

4. I will incorporate more worship into my daily life by:

INDIVIDUAL HEARTWORK – CEDE TO OBEDIENCE TO THE LORD

Write a letter of commitment to the Lord below regarding the area of struggle you are facing. Let Him know that you want all that He has for you.

INDIVIDUAL HEARTWORK – CEDE TO GOD'S LOVE

1. Sit in a quiet place and meditate on His love for several minutes. Ask Him to show you more of His love. Write down or draw below what He shows you.

2. Rate your self on how well you receive His love from 0-10.

3. Write your plan for dwelling more in His love as a daily practice.

INDIVIDUAL HEARTWORK – CEDE TO LISTENING TO YOUR WHOLE SELF

1. Write out your plan below for checking in with your emotions and body daily, inviting Jesus into those sacred spaces.

2. Write out your plan below for integrating self-care and play into your daily schedule, even in small doses.

3. Another place where we need to listen to our "true self" is in the area of grief. Now take time and journal on any place you need to let yourself express grief.

INDIVIDUAL HEARTWORK – CEDE TO A NEW NARRATIVE

1. Reflect on your self-talk and the words you use to describe yourself and your life. What are you currently speaking about yourself? Are you aligning your words with what God's word says about you, such as declaring that you are a princess, a daughter of the King? Take time to develop your new narrative. Embrace the truth of God's word and allow it to saturate every aspect of your being. Dare to believe in the remarkable transformation that awaits as you surrender to this new narrative and embody the radiant truth of your identity as His beloved. Write the truth of who you are and how God is using your story to bring light into the world below.

2. Now, write down twelve positive, Scripture-based statements you will declare over yourself daily. (e.g., "I am right with God through Jesus.")

INDIVIDUAL HEARTWORK – CEDE TO JOY

I invite you to reflect on the possibility and reality of walking in joy every day. Take a moment in your *Heart Journey*™ *Journal* below to contemplate the transformative power of joy in your life. Consider how the joy of the Lord can infuse strength into each step you take, even when facing challenges. Embrace the truth that joy is not just a fleeting visitor, but a permanent resident in your heart as you surrender to the abundant joy that God offers. Journal on your commitment to walk in more joy by staring at Jesus, being filled with Him, and only glancing at life's difficulties.

Next, enjoy this Radiant Memories Activity.

RADIANT MEMORIES ACTIVITY

At times, a source of joy can come from positive experiences. Through this Radiant Memories Activity we will access a positive memory and deepen our awareness of Jesus in that place. We are going to practice staying with a positive memory and good feelings. After working with our traumas, we have more capacity to stay with the positive. Be careful to not let anything negative in, but try to stay with the positive. That is a skill a healthy nervous system can do.

Find a quiet and comfortable space where you can relax and be free from distractions. Take a few deep breaths to center yourself in the presence of God.

Begin by reflecting on your life, specifically focusing on your childhood. As you intentionally clear away negative thoughts, invite God to reveal positive memories that may have been forgotten or overlooked. Trust that He will guide you to the memories that bring joy and gratitude.

Allow yourself to be open to God's Presence as you recall a positive memory from your childhood. It could be a small moment of love, acceptance, or freedom. Embrace the feeling associated with that memory, recognizing it as a precious blessing from God.

As you immerse yourself in that positive memory, become aware of the sensations in your body. Notice how your body responds to the experience of love, acceptance, or freedom. Allow yourself to fully embrace and enjoy these sensations, acknowledging them as gifts from God.

Soften your heart even more, surrendering to the beauty and positivity of this memory. Let go of any resistance or fear, and fully immerse yourself in the presence of God's love and blessings. Feel His arms around you, comforting and nurturing you in this sacred moment.

Take a moment to express your gratitude to God for the positive memory and His continued presence in your life. Offer a prayer of thanksgiving, acknowledging His goodness and faithfulness.

Carry the essence of this positive memory and the awareness of God's love with you throughout your day. Whenever you encounter challenges or negativity, recall this memory and draw strength from it, knowing that God's blessings surround you.

Use this QR code to access audible versions of activities.

INDIVIDUAL HEARTWORK – RECLAIMING LOST OPPORTUNITIES
RECLAIMING LOST OPPORTUNITIES EXERCISE 1

Think back in your life, especially to your childhood, regarding what you wish you would have had but did not have the opportunity (e.g., a loving community, a particular skill, a certain experience, etc.). You might even go back to the "Narrate Your Story" notes and consider what you wish you would have had earlier in life that you did not have. Write this "wish" in column one.

In column two, make a list of "re-do" activities, where you can give those things to yourself. This is where we act, moving out of learned helplessness and saying, "I can do something about this. I can!" So, what is it that you wanted to do? Learn to dance? It is not too late to take a dance lesson. Or you can ask someone at church to teach you how to do something if money is tight. As you review your list of "re-do" activities, it will become clear where you can get back what the enemy stole from you. God makes it clear that He will give us back what the enemy took. "For I will restore health to you and heal you of your wounds," says the Lord … (Jeremiah 30:17, NKJV).

In column three, write the date by which you will engage in the re-do activity. After each re-do activity, come back to column four and record what you felt before, during, and after the re-do activity. This experience is quite redemptive, where you take back what the spiritual enemy took from you.

The fourth column is where you will journal what it was like to "re-do" the activity. Deborah recalls when she played tennis with a group of people, and she felt so insecure. All her adolescent insecurities came back. But she overcame it, and you can, too.

In My Earlier Life, I Wish I Had More:	My Re-do Activity	Date Due	What Was My Re-Do Like?

RECLAIMING LOST OPPORTUNITIES EXERCISE 2

In this exercise, we not only focus on replacing anxiety with faith but also recognize that by doing so, we are participating with Jesus in reclaiming the opportunities that were lost. As we trust in God and let go of fear, we open ourselves to His restoration and the abundance He desires for us.

By taking the time to imagine what life would be like without fear and embracing faith instead, we create a mindset of possibility and hope. This shift in perspective allows us to see the potential for restoration and the fulfillment of the opportunities that were once lost. Even from a natural standpoint, living with less fear and more confidence opens doors to new experiences and growth. However, when we add God to the equation, our lives are empowered and transformed in ways we cannot even fathom. Faith is a currency of heaven; it makes kingdom miracles happen.

In the chart provided, write down ten things you are afraid of in the first column. This exercise serves as a starting point for identifying the areas where fear has held you back. In the second column, craft faith statements that directly counteract each fear, using the Word of God as your foundation. These faith statements remind us of the promises and assurances God has given us in His Word.

Make it a daily practice to meditate on these faith statements in the second column. By immersing ourselves in the truth of God's promises, we allow His word to renew our minds and strengthen our faith. As you meditate on these statements, visualize yourself stepping out in faith, free from the grip of fear, and seizing the restored opportunities before you.

In addition, memorize this Scripture: "I can do all things through Christ who strengthens me" (Philippians 4:13, NKJV). This verse reminds us that our ability to overcome fear and accomplish great things comes from the strength we receive through Christ.

By actively replacing anxiety with faith and aligning our thoughts and actions with God's promises, we position ourselves to experience the restoration of lost opportunities. Trusting in God's guidance and provision, we can step out of our small comfort zones, embrace new delightful challenges, and reclaim the blessings and opportunities that were once pilfered from us. As we journey through this exercise, we invite the transformative work of the Holy Spirit to lead us into a life that is abundant, purposeful, and filled with the joy of reclaiming what was lost.

My Old Fear	My New Faith Statement

RECLAIMING LOST OPPORTUNITIES EXERCISE 3

You have been given this life: own it, live it, and make it what you want it to be. Follow the Lord in it, but enjoy it. We have cleared much of that trauma wreckage away from your restored heart, and now it is time to own your life! God means for you to enjoy it.

I have included my Big List of Enjoyable Activity Options, which has almost two hundred activities for your enjoyment. There is so much we can do to enjoy our lives. We have our Mind Mansion™, where there are millions of different "thought rooms" we could go into. In this beautiful journey of life, you have been given the precious gift of existence. It is yours to own, to live, and to shape into what you desire it to be. As you walk in the footsteps of the Lord, remember to find joy in every moment. Circle or highlight all the activities on the list that you might enjoy and make time to do them!

DR. BARBARA'S BIG LIST OF ENJOYABLE ACTIVITIES

Hike	Ride a bike
Shopping/window shopping	Build a fort with a child
Puzzles	Sightsee
Manicure	Pedicure
Spa day	Take pictures
Spend time with animals	Spend time with safe friends
Hug	Go for a joy ride
Plan a bounce trip	Pick flowers
Make a new board on social media	Sit in a hammock
Swim	People watch
Write a story	Make up a new recipe

Play sports	Bake for someone
Volunteer	Learn an instrument
Start a collection	Craft
Visit a museum	Visit model homes
Go on a hayride	Take a cooking class
Take a craft class	Make a vison board
Collage	Listen to an audiobook
Take a bubble bath	Light scented candles
Grow an herb garden	Plant flowers
Buy a Bonsai tree	Attend a local festival
Go to a local reading/poetry throw-down	Talk with an accent all day
See live music	Create a treasure hunt
Take a dance class	Have a Princess Party
Visit an out of town friend	Visit an out of town relative
Go on a cruise	Spend time with animals
Spend time with kids	Watch funny videos
Watch a new sitcom	Go to a movie
Ride a horse	Visit a farm
Take kids to a sing-along	Go out to eat
Shop at a thrift store	Walk around a lake
Visit a state park	Camp

Make a bonfire	Make s'mores
Make jewelry	Visit antique stores
Visit a nearby town	Checkout historical sites nearby
Visit IKEA (day-long activity!)	Journal about your goals
Read 20 New Testament Scriptures on	Watch funny YouTube videos
God's Love	Scan old pictures into Facebook
Start a YouTube channel	Play board games
Go on a date	Exercise
Play video games	Re-read a favorite book
Stretch your muscles	Zip-line
Binge on Ted Talks	Live a day without guilt
Pretend you have no fear for a day	Jump on a trampoline
Write a short story	Go to the zoo
Visit an amusement park	Learn to knit
Visit an aquarium	Worship and praise the Lord
Draw or paint	Memorize a promise Scripture
Make a gratitude list	Discover local flora at an arboretum
Perform an unseen act of kindness	Attend a sporting event
Visit a university	Get a massage
Watch a comedy show	Give to the homeless
Adopt a rescue animal	Discover your spiritual gifts

Study a new language	Show kindness to a stranger
Join a Bible study	Call a friend you have not spoken to in a while
Go to a petting zoo	Clean out a closet
Give yourself a homemade facial	Throw a party
Try a new hairstyle	Go to Meet-up
Visit a support group	Start a dinner club
Try a new food dish/genre	Buy a new outfit for under $50
Join a book club	Play Pokémon Go
Geocache	Have a yard sale
Buy and use a unique kitchen utensil	Visit the flea market
Go to a yard sale	Study local history
Study your genealogy	Play hide and go seek with kids
Make amends with someone	Write your memoirs
Write a short story	Write poetry
Read poetry	Go to a pawn shop
Take a photography class	Donate to Goodwill
Go to the Dollar Store	Text all your friends an encouragement
Support a ministry with time or money	Write a song
Have a game night	Try wood or metal working

Listen to music	Attend a play
Attend a concert	Start a side hustle business
Sing Karaoke	Buy a new skin care product
Buy pretty lingerie for yourself	Go parasailing
Start a new hobby	Ride a 4-wheeler
Go skydiving	Be an extra on a TV show or movie
Learn a new sport	Write letters to those who seem lonely
Hand write letters to loved ones	Host a luau
Throw a surprise "just because we love you" party	Host a tea party
Handmake Christmas ornaments	Try a new coffee or specialty drink
Have high tea with friends at a tea shop	Make a cozy fire
Shop at a vintage clothing store	Kiss or dance in the rain
Make a bucket list	Make a seasonal wreath
Make snow cream	Raise money for a charity
Take a class at a local college	Visit the sick
Run (or walk) a 5K	Plan your dream trip
Visit the elderly	Paint a room
Start a gratitude journal	Buy a card for someone, just because …

Read old cards/letters from your spouse	Go to the mountains
Go to the beach	Attend a retreat
Go to a waterpark	Renew your vows
Plan girls' trip	Go through mementos
Create a mementos box	Video record your aging relatives' memories
Video your memoirs	Run barefoot in the grass
Lay in the grass	Visit a state park
Visit the local library	Have a pajama day
Listen to new music	Go to a drive-in move
Buy yourself a stuffed animal	Try out for a play
Rent a convertible for a weekend	

INDIVIDUAL HEARTWORK – CHAPTER TEN REVIEW

Reflect on and journal your answers to the below questions.

1. What are some hopes, dreams, and lost opportunities you missed over the years?

2. Which one or ones do you hold closest to your heart that you would like to "re-do"? Write out practical ways to get you started down that path.

3. Which of the ceding exercises and categories resonated most with you?

4. How can you begin incorporating those into your life?

5. Think of at least three way you can invite Jesus into these rooms when you become weary and fearful. How might you keep yourself in check and in balance? Share this with your accountability or prayer partner for support.

HEART GROUP DISCUSSION – TIME TO SHARE.

1. As you prayed and went through this lesson, what was the toughest part for you? Were you able to work through it? Share with your group or safe person so they can lift it up in prayer.

2. How did you feel at the beginning of this lesson before realizing you could restore lost opportunities? How do you feel now?

3. What are some special insights about your heart home did Jesus share with you as you began to yield to Him even more?

4. As you continue on this Heart Journey™, what are you most excited about and why?

5. What are you least excited about? Share your responses with your group and/or prayer and accountability partner, as well as how they can pray for in this area.

Keystone Scriptures for
Restoring My Lost Opportunities

NOW MEMORIZE THESE KEYSTONE SCRIPTURES:

Then the Lord your God will restore your fortunes and have compassion on you and gather you again from all the nations where He scattered you.

Deuteronomy 30:3 (AMP)

Forget the former things; do not dwell on the past. See, I am doing a new thing! Now it springs up; do you not perceive it? I am making a way in the wilderness and streams in the wasteland.

Isaiah 43:18-19 (AMP)

As you know, we count as blessed those who have persevered. You have heard of Job's perseverance and have seen what the Lord finally brought about. The Lord is full of compassion and mercy.

James 5:11 (AMP)

LET US PRAY.

Heavenly Father,

You have done such an amazing work in our heart home during this journey. We have learned so much about ourselves—every part of our beings, how life experiences affected us, and how we can become and remain overcomers. Thank You, Father, for walking with us on this journey. May our hearts and minds continue to be open to Your heart's desire for every aspect of our lives, and may we continue to embrace Your healing touch.

In Jesus' name, Amen.

Chapter

ELEVEN

RESTORING MY PURPOSE

Instead of your shame you will receive a double portion, and instead of disgrace you will rejoice in your inheritance. And so you will inherit a double portion in your land, and everlasting joy will be yours.

Isaiah 61:7 (NIV)

SUPPLIES

For this chapter's Heartwork, you will need a pen or pencil and your *Heart Journey™ Journal*, old magazines, markers or colored pencils, glue, and scissors. Posterboard is optional.

INDIVIDUAL HEARTWORK – VISION BOARD: CHRISTIAN VERSION

For this activity, gather your journal, pen or pencil, markers or colored pencils, old magazines, scissors, glue, and any other materials you want to use for creating a vision board or poster. You will use the space below or you can even purchase a poster board.

As we embark on this expedition of discovering our purpose, let us remain open to the leading of the Holy Spirit. Through prayer and meditation, we invite Him to reveal the unique destiny He has designed for each of us. It is important to remember that our purpose is intricately woven into the very fabric of our being, embedded within our DNA by God Himself.

Now, let us transition to the exciting process of creating our vision boards. As you flip through magazines or other resources, be attentive to the prompting of the Holy Spirit. Cut out images, words, and symbols that resonate with your heart and reflect the dreams and aspirations planted within you by the Holy Spirit. Take your time with this step, allowing God to guide you in selecting the elements that truly speak to your soul.

In case you cannot find exactly what you are looking for, do not hesitate to use your artistic skills. You can use markers or colored pencils to draw or even print out clip art that aligns with your vision. Remember, your vision board is not a random assortment of desires, but a tangible reflection of the specific calling God has placed on your life.

As you curate your vision board, trust that God is using this activity to reveal His plan and purpose for you. Expect the astonishing and anticipate that His vision for your life will surpass anything you could ask or envisage. This creative process is a partnership with the Holy Spirit, allowing Him to decode and illuminate the path ahead.

Let your vision board be a visual representation of the divine calling upon your life. It serves as a powerful reminder of the dreams and aspirations God has placed in your heart. By aligning ourselves with His purpose and surrendering to His leading, we position ourselves to walk in the abundant life He has prepared for us. So, let us embrace this activity with faith and anticipation, knowing that God is guiding our steps and unveiling His extraordinary plans for our lives.

1. Create your vision board on the next page.

My Vision Board with Jesus

2. Now write a summary of what you learned through your Vision Board with Jesus. If you were to summarize your Vision Board with Jesus into a paragraph, what would you say about your purpose? Write this below.

3. Now take time to journal and reflect on a 10x God-sized vision for your life. Consider what it would look like for your purpose to be multiplied 10x by the power of God. Write down your thoughts, dreams, and prayers as you surrender your vision to Him, trusting that He can do exceedingly abundantly above all that you can ask or imagine (Ephesians 3:20).

4. Now take time to journal and reflect on a 100x God-sized vision for your life. Yep, that was not a typo! Consider what it would look like for your purpose to be multiplied 100x by the power and reach of God. Write down your thoughts, dreams, and prayers as you surrender your vision to Him, trusting that He can do exceedingly abundantly above all that you can ask or imagine (Ephesians 3:20).

INDIVIDUAL HEARTWORK – GOD'S PURPOSE WOVEN THROUGH TIME

In the intricate tapestry of your life, every environmental experience you have encountered has been delicately woven together, and God intends to use all of it. When you find yourself in that sweet spot of fulfilling your calling, you will experience an overwhelming sense of peace and flow. It is a profound realization that "I was made to do this." I have witnessed countless individuals discovering this truth and taking flight into purpose, and I believe you, too, will lift into this glorious flight, Beloved.

Let us commence this introspective exploration from the very beginning, the early years of zero to six or from birth through kindergarten. Although memories from this period may be faint, reflect upon your interests, the stories you have heard about yourself, your favorite toys, and your temperament. Were you shy, easygoing, or strong-willed? Take a moment to write down what you can recall.

1. From ages zero to five years, write down what you know about/remember:

   a. Your interests:

   b. Your favorite things:

   c. Your temperaments (e.g., curious, strong-willed, stubborn, calm, sensitive, expressive, playful, etc. All traits are gifts and part of your design)

2. Moving forward, let us delve into the elementary school years, encompassing ages six through ten. What activities brought you immense joy during this time? If given free time, what were your favorite toys and activities? What did you genuinely love to do? Did you prefer solitude or being in the company of others? Did you enjoy large groups, small gatherings, or one-on-one interactions? Reflect on your strength of will. Were you easy-

going, strong-willed, or somewhere in between? Think about the people you loved to be around and why. Moreover, ponder the topics or undertakings that captivated your attention.

As far as reporting on personality traits, here are some examples:

a. Curiosity: Showing a natural inclination to explore and seek knowledge.

b. Empathy: Demonstrating a strong ability to understand and share the feelings of others.

c. Leadership: Displaying qualities that inspire and guide others toward a common goal.

d. Perseverance: Exhibiting determination and resilience in the face of challenges.

e. Creativity: Having a knack for generating unique ideas and thinking outside the box.

f. Analytical: Possessing a logical and systematic approach to problem-solving.

g. Optimism: Maintaining a positive outlook and seeing possibilities in every situation.

h. Compassion: Showing deep concern and care for the well-being of others.

i. Adaptability: Being flexible and open to change, easily adjusting to new circumstances.

j. Organization: Having a natural inclination toward order and structure.

k. Intuition: Trusting one's instincts and relying on inner guidance.

l. Assertiveness: Being confident in expressing ideas and standing up for oneself.

m. Diplomacy: Navigating conflicts with tact and sensitivity, seeking peaceful resolutions.

n. Introspection: Engaging in deep self-reflection and introspective practices.

o. Reliability: Being dependable and fulfilling commitments consistently.

p. Attention to detail: Noticing and focusing on the finer aspects of tasks or situations.

q. Humility: Maintaining a modest and humble demeanor, acknowledging one's limitations.

r. Adaptability: Being able to adjust to different environments and work well with diverse groups.

s. Initiative: Taking proactive steps and showing a willingness to take on responsibilities.

t. Assertiveness: Expressing thoughts and needs with confidence and clarity.

u. Patience: Demonstrating the ability to wait calmly and endure challenging circumstances.

v. Resilience: Bouncing back from setbacks and finding strength in adversity.

w. Teamwork: Thriving in collaborative settings and valuing collective achievement.

x. Attention to detail: Having an eye for precision and maintaining high standards.

y. Visionary: Possessing the ability to see possibilities and envision a better future.

3. From ages six to ten years (elementary school years), write down what you remember:

    a.   Your interests:

    b.   Your favorite possessions:

    c.   Your favorite activities:

    d.   Your temperaments/personality traits:

    e.   Your talents:

    f.   Your favorite subjects:

g. Who did you like to be with? (types of people, groups, or crowds vs. alone time, etc.)

As we progress, consider the emergence of other talents and personality traits during your middle school years. Address the same questions as before, focusing on what you enjoyed adding to your life. Reflect on the classes, clubs, or extracurricular activities that ignited your passion. Identify your strengths and the subjects in which you excelled. What did you love discussing? Unearth your deepest passions and interests. Consider whether you thrived in large groups, small gatherings, or if you leaned toward being an extrovert, introvert, or somewhere in between. Did you find fulfillment in deep contemplation or in engaging with a diverse range of people and topics? Write down your thoughts, capturing the essence of this transformative period.

4. From ages eleven to fourteen years (middle school years), write down what you remember:

a. Your interests:

b. Your favorite possessions:

c. Your favorite activities:

d.   Your temperaments/personality traits:

e.   Your talents:

f.   Your favorite subjects/classes/clubs:

g.   Who did you like to be with? (types of people, groups, or crowds vs. alone time, etc.)

Now, let us transition into the high school years, encompassing ages fourteen through eighteen. Recall your interests during this time, and reflect upon your temperament. Contemplate the things you genuinely enjoyed. Did a hunger for travel arise once you entered the workforce or higher education? Consider whether you gravitated toward routines or preferred a multitude of experiences and variety. Consider the courses you enjoyed, the extracurricular activities that resonated with you, and the social and academic environments in which you thrived. Explore how you spent your free time during this stage of life. Furthermore, ponder the scenarios that captivated your attention. Take a moment to document these reflections.

5. From ages fourteen to eighteen years (high school years), write down what you remember:

   a.   Your interests:

   b.   Your favorite possessions:

   c.   Your favorite activities:

   d.   Your temperaments/personality traits:

   e.   Your talents:

   f.   Your favorite subjects/classes/clubs:

g. Who did you like to be with? (types of people, groups, or crowds vs. alone time, etc.)

h. What interested you on the job in school or about the world?

Now we will extend this exercise into your adulthood and up until the present day, examining what activities and pursuits you love, where your passion lies, and which job duties resonate deeply with you. Identify the moments when you felt like you were truly in your element, experiencing a sense of ease and joy. These instances likely align with what you were made for, where your natural talents and inclinations flourished. Remember, sometimes what brings you fulfillment may seem challenging to others, but it is uniquely your sweet spot.

In addition, reflect on how some of your past traumas have been transformed into sources of passion and calling. Consider personal experiences, which evoked deep emotions and empathy within you. Reflect on how you have channeled that compassion into a fulfilling career, ministry of life.

6. From ages eighteen-current year, inventory the following:

a. Your interests:

b. Your favorite possessions:

c. Your favorite activities:

d. Your temperaments/personality traits:

e. Your talents:

f. Your favorite subjects/classes/clubs:

g. Who did you like to be with? (types of people, groups, or crowds vs. alone time, etc.)

h. What interested you on the job or about the world?

Now, take time to reflect on the inventory you completed above, capturing your interests, favorite things, preferences, passions, temperaments, and the like throughout different stages of your life. Now, let us explore the threads of continuity and purpose that may be woven into your unique journey.

7. Grab some colored markers or crayons and use them to visually represent the connections you find. Here's how you can approach it:

    a. Circle the words or draw lines through different colors: As you review your inventory, identify recurring themes, interests, or personality traits. Circle the words or draw lines connecting related items using different colors. For example, if you notice a pattern of creativity, use one color to connect all instances of creative interests or talents.

    b. Key code: Create a key code at the top of your page to help you interpret the colors and symbols you use. Assign each color or symbol a specific meaning or theme. This will make it easier to understand the connections you are diagraming.

    c. Identify threads of continuity: Look for patterns, overlaps, or commonalities across different stages of your life. Are there particular interests or traits that consistently appear throughout your journey? Are there any significant shifts or transformations that stand out? Take note of these threads of continuity.

    d. Reflect on God's purpose: As you examine the threads you have identified; consider how they might relate to God's plan for your life. Reflect on how these patterns and traits may align with your unique purpose and the ways in which God has woven them into your journey.

e. Take your time: This exercise may require some contemplation and introspection. Give yourself the space and time needed to explore and understand the connections fully. Allow your thoughts and insights to flow as you engage with the visual representation of your journey.

Remember, this exercise is intended to help you uncover potential threads of purpose that God has woven throughout your life. Embrace the process of discovery and be open to new insights that may arise. Enjoy the journey of exploring your unique calling and how your experiences and traits contribute to the tapestry of your life.

8. Write below what you have been shown about your calling:

a. I was made with these passions and interests:

b. I was created to minister in these situations/ I am drawn to ministering in these settings:

c. I do best with these supports:

d. When I serve the world through and with Jesus, I use these talents:

e. I have been equipped to serve in these ways:

f. I was created with this temperament:

g. My temperament helps me to serve in this way:

h. I have a passion for those who have been through these traumas and trials:

INDIVIDUAL HEARTWORK - MY SPIRITUAL GIFTS

1. Read 1 Corinthians 12, 13, and 14. In particular, pay attention to the spiritual gifts. Write what you learned about spiritual gifts.

2. Now circle the top five spiritual gifts that you see in yourself.

   a. Administration - 1 Corinthians 12:28 (NIV): "those with gifts of administration."

   b. Apostleship* - Ephesians 4:11(NIV): "So Christ Himself gave the apostles."

   c. Creative communication - Exodus 31:3-5(NIV): "I have filled him with the Spirit of God, with wisdom, with understanding, with knowledge and with all kinds of skills."

   d. Deliverance - Mark 16:17 (NIV): "And these signs will accompany those who believe: In My name, they will drive out demons."

   e. Discipleship - Matthew 28:19-20 (NIV): "Therefore go and make disciples of all nations."

   f. Distinguishing between spirits – 1 Corinthians 12:8 (NIV): "to another distinguishing between spirits."

   g. Encouragement - Romans 12:8 (NIV): "if it is to encourage, then give encouragement."

   h. Evangelism - Ephesians 4:11 (NIV): "So Christ Himself gave the apostles, the prophets, the evangelists."

i. Faith - 1 Corinthians 12:9 (NIV): "to another faith."

j. Giving - Romans 12:8 (NIV): "if it is to give, do it generously."

k. Healing - 1 Corinthians 12:9 (NIV): "gifts of healing."

l. Helps - 1 Corinthians 12:28 (NIV): "those able to help others."

m. Hospitality - Romans 12:13 (NIV): "Practice hospitality."

n. Intercession - Romans 8:26 (NIV): "The Spirit helps us in our weakness. We do not know what we ought to pray for, but the Spirit Himself intercedes for us through wordless groans."

o. Interpretation of tongues* - 1 Corinthians 12:10 (NIV): "to another the interpretation of tongues."

p. Knowledge - 1 Corinthians 12:8 (NIV): "to another a message of knowledge."

q. Leadership - Romans 12:8 (NIV): "if it is to lead, do it diligently."

r. Mercy - Romans 12:8 (NIV): "if it is to show mercy, do it cheerfully."

s. Miracles* - 1 Corinthians 12:10 (NIV): "to another miraculous powers."

t. Music/worship - 1 Chronicles 25:1-3 (NIV): "to prophesy accompanied by the lyres, harps, and cymbals."

u. Pastoring/Shepherding - Ephesians 4:11 (NIV): "So Christ Himself gave the apostles, the prophets, the evangelists, the pastors and teachers."

v. Prophecy* - 1 Corinthians 12:10 (NIV): "to another prophecy."

w. Serving - 1 Peter 4:10-11 (NIV): "Each of you should use whatever gift you have received to serve others."

x. Teaching - Romans 12:7 (NIV): "if it is teaching, then teach."

y. Tongues* - 1 Corinthians 12:10 (NIV): "to another speaking in different kinds of tongues."

z.   Wisdom - 1 Corinthians 12:8 (NIV): "to another the message of wisdom."

Note: Some denominations believe that certain gifts, marked with an asterisk, have passed away or are not actively present in the Church today. These beliefs vary among different theological perspectives.

Next, you will ask two friends or family members who are safe spiritually mature others and who know you well to circle the top five spiritual gifts they see in you.

3.   Next, ask one of the friends or family members to circle the top five spiritual gifts he or she sees in you.

a.   Administration - 1 Corinthians 12:28 (NIV): "those with gifts of administration."

b.   Apostleship* - Ephesians 4:11(NIV): "So Christ Himself gave the apostles."

c.   Creative communication - Exodus 31:3-5(NIV): "I have filled him with the Spirit of God, with wisdom, with understanding, with knowledge and with all kinds of skills."

d.   Deliverance - Mark 16:17 (NIV): "And these signs will accompany those who believe: In my name, they will drive out demons."

e.   Discipleship - Matthew 28:19-20 (NIV): "Therefore go and make disciples of all nations."

f.   Distinguishing between spirits – 1 Corinthians 12:8 (NIV): "to another distinguishing between spirits."

g.   Encouragement - Romans 12:8 (NIV): "if it is to encourage, then give encouragement."

h.   Evangelism - Ephesians 4:11 (NIV): "So Christ Himself gave the apostles, the prophets, the evangelists."

i.   Faith - 1 Corinthians 12:9 (NIV): "to another faith."

j.   Giving - Romans 12:8 (NIV): "if it is to give, do it generously."

k.   Healing - 1 Corinthians 12:9 (NIV): "gifts of healing."

l.   Helps - 1 Corinthians 12:28 (NIV): "those able to help others."

m. Hospitality - Romans 12:13 (NIV): "Practice hospitality."

n.   Intercession - Romans 8:26 (NIV): "The Spirit helps us in our weakness. We do not know what we ought to pray for, but the Spirit Himself intercedes for us through wordless groans."

o.   Interpretation of tongues* - 1 Corinthians 12:10 (NIV): "to another the interpretation of tongues."

p.   Knowledge - 1 Corinthians 12:8 (NIV): "to another a message of knowledge."

q.   Leadership - Romans 12:8 (NIV): "if it is to lead, do it diligently."

r.   Mercy - Romans 12:8 (NIV): "if it is to show mercy, do it cheerfully."

s.   Miracles* - 1 Corinthians 12:10 (NIV): "to another miraculous powers."

t.   Music/worship - 1 Chronicles 25:1-3 (NIV): "to prophesy accompanied by the lyres, harps, and cymbals."

u.   Pastoring/Shepherding - Ephesians 4:11 (NIV): "So Christ Himself gave the apostles, the prophets, the evangelists, the pastors and teachers."

v.   Prophecy* - 1 Corinthians 12:10 (NIV): "to another prophecy."

w. Serving - 1 Peter 4:10-11 (NIV): "Each of you should use whatever gift you have received to serve others."

x.   Teaching - Romans 12:7 (NIV): "if it is teaching, then teach."

y.   Tongues* - 1 Corinthians 12:10 (NIV): "to another speaking in different kinds of tongues."

z.   Wisdom - 1 Corinthians 12:8 (NIV): "to another the message of wisdom."

*Note: Some denominations believe that certain gifts, marked with an asterisk, have passed away or are not actively present in the Church today. These beliefs vary among different theological perspectives.

4. Now ask the other friend or family member to circle the top five spiritual gifts he or she sees in you.

   a. Administration - 1 Corinthians 12:28 (NIV): "those with gifts of administration."

   b. Apostleship* - Ephesians 4:11(NIV): "So Christ Himself gave the apostles."

   c. Creative communication - Exodus 31:3-5(NIV): "I have filled him with the Spirit of God, with wisdom, with understanding, with knowledge and with all kinds of skills."

   d. Deliverance - Mark 16:17 (NIV): "And these signs will accompany those who believe: In my name, they will drive out demons."

   e. Discipleship - Matthew 28:19-20 (NIV): "Therefore go and make disciples of all nations."

   f. Distinguishing between spirits – 1 Corinthians 12:8 (NIV): "to another distinguishing between spirits."

   g. Encouragement - Romans 12:8 (NIV): "if it is to encourage, then give encouragement."

   h. Evangelism - Ephesians 4:11 (NIV): "So Christ Himself gave the apostles, the prophets, the evangelists."

   i. Faith - 1 Corinthians 12:9 (NIV): "to another faith."

   j. Giving - Romans 12:8 (NIV): "if it is to give, do it generously."

   k. Healing - 1 Corinthians 12:9 (NIV): "gifts of healing."

   l. Helps - 1 Corinthians 12:28 (NIV): "those able to help others."

   m. Hospitality - Romans 12:13 (NIV): "Practice hospitality."

   n. Intercession - Romans 8:26 (NIV): "The Spirit helps us in our weakness. We do not know what we ought to pray for, but the Spirit Himself intercedes for us through wordless groans."

   o. Interpretation of tongues* - 1 Corinthians 12:10 (NIV): "to another the interpretation of tongues."

p.   Knowledge - 1 Corinthians 12:8 (NIV): "to another a message of knowledge."

q.   Leadership - Romans 12:8 (NIV): "if it is to lead, do it diligently."

r.   Mercy - Romans 12:8 (NIV): "if it is to show mercy, do it cheerfully."

s.   Miracles* - 1 Corinthians 12:10 (NIV): "to another miraculous powers."

t.   Music/worship - 1 Chronicles 25:1-3 (NIV): "to prophesy accompanied by the lyres, harps, and cymbals."

u.   Pastoring/Shepherding - Ephesians 4:11 (NIV): "So Christ Himself gave the apostles, the prophets, the evangelists, the pastors and teachers."

v.   Prophecy* - 1 Corinthians 12:10 (NIV): "to another prophecy."

w.   Serving - 1 Peter 4:10-11 (NIV): "Each of you should use whatever gift you have received to serve others."

x.   Teaching - Romans 12:7 (NIV): "if it is teaching, then teach."

y.   Tongues* - 1 Corinthians 12:10 (NIV): "to another speaking in different kinds of tongues."

z.   Wisdom - 1 Corinthians 12:8 (NIV): "to another the message of wisdom."

*Note: Some denominations believe that certain gifts, marked with an asterisk, have passed away or are not actively present in the Church today. These beliefs vary among different theological perspectives.

5. Take the time to delve into the inventories mentioned above and, in addition, seek the guidance of the Lord to discern the unique gifts He has bestowed upon you. Write down your top five spiritual gifts below.

Next, we will explore the biblical principles of faithfulness, obedience, and the development of talents, drawing inspiration from the remarkable lives of Billy Graham and Ann Graham Lotz. By examining their journeys, we will understand the importance of recognizing and utilizing our gifts for the fulfillment of God's extraordinary dreams for us. Remember, 1 Peter 4:10 (NIV) says, "Each of you should use whatever gift you have received to serve others, as faithful stewards of God's grace in its various forms.

The late Billy Graham was a renowned evangelist and preacher who impacted millions of lives with the message of the Gospel. From a young age, Graham felt a deep calling to share God's love and embarked on a lifelong journey of faithfulness to that calling. He dedicated his time to studying the Scriptures, honing his speaking skills, and continuously developing his God-given gift of communication. Graham's dedication to utilizing his talents led to numerous opportunities, including the founding of the Billy Graham Evangelistic Association and the organization of large-scale evangelistic crusades around the world. Through his unwavering obedience and faithful stewardship of his gift, he witnessed countless individuals finding salvation and hope in Christ. The story of Billy Graham reminds us that by nurturing and using our talents faithfully, we can have a profound impact on the world and fulfill God's purpose for our lives.

Ann Graham Lotz, the daughter of Billy Graham, is a prominent author, teacher, speaker, and evangelist. Inspired by her father's faith and passion for the Gospel, Ann discovered her own unique gift of teaching and communicating bib-

lical truths. She embraced her personal calling and dedicated herself to deepening her knowledge of the Scriptures and honing her speaking, writing, and teaching abilities. Through her ministry, Lotz has touched the lives of innumerable individuals around the world, encouraging them to deepen their relationship with God and seek His presence. Her faithfulness and obedience in utilizing her gift have led to transformative experiences and have enabled her to inspire others to follow Christ wholeheartedly.

6. Now pray and ask Jesus what His plan is for you regarding stewarding your gifts and write out your plan below:

   a. My plan for and commitment to faithfulness and obedience:

   b. My plan for and commitment to make an impact through stewardship:

INDIVIDUAL HEARTWORK – MY PURPOSE STATEMENT

Now let us complete your Purpose Statement.

1. I was made with these passions and interests:

2. I was created to minister in these situations/ I am drawn to ministering in these settings:

3. I do best with these supports:

4. When I serve the world through and with Jesus, I use these talents:

5. I have been equipped to serve in these ways:

6. I was created with this temperament:

7. My temperament helps me to serve in this way:

8. I serve with the following spiritual gifts:

9. I have a passion for those who have been through these traumas and trials:

10. I feel His pleasure when:

Now, combine all the above into a paragraph that states what your purpose is.

For example, Billy Graham's Purpose Statement might be:

My purpose is to passionately proclaim the Gospel, connect with people from all backgrounds, and lead them to a personal relationship with Jesus Christ. I thrive in large gatherings and stadiums, where I can share the message of salvation to vast audiences. With the support of a dedicated team, I utilize my talents of public speaking, leadership, and discernment to effectively communicate God's love and grace. Equipped with charisma, wisdom, and the ability to connect with others, I bridge gaps and break

down barriers, guiding individuals toward a life-transforming encounter with Christ. My humble and compassionate temperament creates a safe space for healing and restoration. Operating in the spiritual gifts of preaching, evangelism, leadership, and discernment, I am passionate about reaching those who have experienced traumas and trials, offering them hope, healing, and a renewed sense of purpose. Ultimately, I find deep joy and fulfillment in witnessing lives transformed and seeing the message of salvation reach hearts on a large scale.

Now it is your turn. Write your Purpose Statement:

OPERATE FROM PURPOSE
INDIVIDUAL HEARTWORK – SHAKE OFF THE DUST

Find a quiet and comfortable space where you can reflect and engage in this exercise without distractions. Have your *Heart Journey*™ *Journal* and a pen ready. Take a few deep breaths, allowing yourself to relax and be present in this moment. Close your eyes if it helps you focus.

1. Answer this question: "What do I need to violently shake off in regard to my purpose?" Allow your mind to freely explore and identify any fears, doubts, negative beliefs, or past failures that have been holding you back from fully embracing your purpose. Write them down without judgment or self-censorship.

2. Take a moment to acknowledge in writing the weight these hindrances have had on your journey. Recognize that you have carried them for long enough and that it is time to release them.

3. Visualize yourself vigorously shaking off the dust from your feet, symbolizing the act of letting go of these limitations. Envision the freedom and liberation that comes from releasing them. Draw this below.

4. Now, in your journal, write a declaration of your determination to shake off the dust. Use empowering language and affirm your faith in God's plan for your life. For example, you could state: "I choose to release these fears, doubts, and negative beliefs that have held me back: _____. I embrace my purpose with unwavering faith, knowing that God has equipped me and goes before me."

5. Reflect on Matthew 10:11-14. Meditate on the words of Jesus encouraging His disciples to leave behind unwelcoming environments and shake off the dust. Consider the relevance of this teaching to your own journey and the importance of not allowing rejection or fear of failure to hinder your purpose.

6. Take a moment to invite the Holy Spirit to guide you through this process. Ask for strength, courage, and discernment as you step into a new season of faith and purpose. Write down what He says to you.

7. As you conclude this exercise, offer a prayer of surrender, releasing any remaining doubts or fears into God's loving hands. Express gratitude for the opportunity to shake off the dust and embrace your purpose with renewed conviction below.

Remember, dear one, this exercise is a powerful step toward embracing your purpose and moving forward in faith. Clasp the process wholeheartedly and trust that God will lead you on a path of purpose, fulfillment, and impact.

Now enjoy this activity: Visualize His Purpose Fulfilled.

Use this QR code to access audible versions of activities.

VISUALIZE HIS PURPOSE FULFILLED ACTIVITY

Find a quiet and comfortable space where you can relax and connect with the Lord. Take a moment to settle into a comfortable position, allowing your body and mind to unwind. Close your eyes and take a few deep breaths in of the breath of God, inhaling Jesus and exhaling any tension or distractions.

I wonder if you would be willing to invite the Lord into this activity. Open your heart and mind to His presence, knowing that He is with you, guiding you in this journey of discovering and embracing your fulfilled purpose.

Now let us visualize yourself stepping into a scene where you are fully aligned with God's purpose for your life. Use your holy imagination to vividly picture yourself in that sweet spot—doing what you are called to do, being all God has designed you to be. See yourself radiating with joy, peace, and fulfillment as you walk in your true purpose.

Imagine Jesus, right there with you, speaking over you, "For I know the plans I have for you," declares the Lord, "plans to prosper you and not to harm you, plans to give you hope and a future." (Jeremiah 29:11, NIV)

In alignment with Jesus, now it is time to speak words of faith and affirmation of your purpose over yourself. Declare aloud the truth of God's promises and His plans for your life. Let your words be filled with conviction and belief, knowing that they carry power to shape your reality. Remember that life is in the power of your tongue, and those who love it will eat its fruits." (Proverbs 18:21, ESV)

Now I wonder if you might surrender any confusion, doubt, or uncertainty to the Lord. Release your worries and fears, and place your trust in His divine guidance and provision. Allow His peace to envelop your heart as you fully trust in His perfect plan for your life. As the Scripture says, "Trust in the Lord with all your heart, and do not lean on your own understanding. In all your ways acknowledge Him, and He will make straight your paths." (Proverbs 3:5-6, ESV)

Now, let's draw our attention to God's timing is perfect. As you visualize your fulfilled purpose, using your eyes of faith which so pleases Jesus, embrace the knowledge that every step, every season, and every experience has led you to this moment. He is at work turning every situation into a good beautiful, purpose-filled place. Surrender any desire to rush or force the process, and instead, rest in the assurance that God's timing will bring forth the fullness of His purpose in your life. As the Scripture says, "For everything there is a season, and a time for every matter under heaven." (Ecclesiastes 3:1, ESV)

Next, I wonder if you can express gratitude to the Lord for His faithfulness and *for the unique purpose, He has imparted within you. With a heart filled with expectation, embrace the journey that lies ahead, knowing that as you continue to seek Him and follow His leading, He will guide you into the fullness of your destiny. Say over yourself, "The Lord will fulfill His purpose for me; your steadfast love, O Lord, endures forever. Do not forsake the work of your hands." (Psalm 138:8, ESV)*

Take a few moments to sit in the presence of the Lord, allowing these visualized images and affirmations permeate your being. When you are ready, slowly open your eyes, carrying with you the confidence and assurance that you are on the path to fulfilling God's purpose for your life.

Use this QR code to access audible versions of activities.

INDIVIDUAL HEARTWORK – OPERATING FROM PURPOSE

Journal on the prompts below.

1. Reflect on your current state of living. Are you fully committed to living on purpose, aligned with God's plan for your life? If not, what factors or obstacles are hindering your commitment? Journal regarding the areas in which you feel disconnected or off course.

2. This week, identify one specific action you can take to move closer to living on purpose. It could be setting aside dedicated time each day for prayer and seeking God's guidance. Ask Him what He wants you to accomplish by His spirit within the week and write this below.

3. Zoom out to the month ahead. Consider what steps you can take to deepen your commitment to living on purpose during this time. It could involve prioritizing spiritual practices, such as reading Scripture, meditating, or attending a faith-based event. Ask Him what He wants you to accomplish by His spirit within the month and write this below.

4. As you enter a new quarter, assess the progress you have made in living on purpose. What adjustments or refinements can you make to further align yourself with God's plan? Ask Him what He wants you to accomplish by His spirit within the quarter and write this below.

5. Looking ahead to the year, envision the transformative impact of committing to on-purpose living. How do you see your life evolving as you align your actions and decisions with God's will? Ask Him what He wants you to accomplish by His spirit within a year and write this below.

6. Spend dedicated time in prayer, seeking God's wisdom and guidance in living on purpose. Ask Him to reveal any areas of your life that need realignment or course correction. Journal about any insights or messages you receive during this prayerful time, noting how you can apply them to your daily life.

7. Look even further ahead, five years into the future. Imagine the growth and transformation that can occur as you continue to seek the Lord's direction in your life. How do you see yourself impacting others and fulfilling your purpose? Ask Him what He wants you to accomplish by His Spirit within five years and write this below.

8. Now, stretch your holy imagination to ten years into the future. Envision the incredible journey you will have undertaken in seeking the Lord's direction and living on purpose. What legacy do you aspire to leave behind? How do you see your life and the lives of those around you transformed by your commitment to God's plan? Ask Him what He wants you to accomplish by His spirit within ten years and write this below.

9. Commit to a regular practice of seeking His guidance intentionally regarding the fulfillment of your purpose. Dedicate time each day, week, or month for prayer and reflection. Journal about your experiences of seeking the Lord's direction and how His guidance has shaped your decisions and actions. Note any patterns or themes that emerge, and use them as anchors for your ongoing commitment to living on purpose. Write your dedication to this practice below.

INDIVIDUAL HEARTWORK – NAVIGATING RELATIONSHIP ANEW

1. List your top five values that you want to live from, while navigating relationships in your life.

2. Reflect on how core negative image is working in your most significant relationships. Also reflect on how you can step out of core negative image. Write below.

3. List how Gottman's four horsemen are working in your relationships and how you can shift these patterns by using the antidotes.

4. Describe five ways you can increase positive sentiment in your primary relationships.

Now enjoy this activity.

GOD-FILLED RELATIONSHIPS ACTIVITY

Find a comfortable position as you prepare for this time with Jesus. Take a moment to focus on your breath, inhaling the breath of God, and exhaling any tension or distractions. As you enter a state of calmness, tap into your holy imagination, as mentioned in Philippians 4:8. Welcome Jesus into this place with you and ask Him to pour His love into you.

As He pours His love into you, imagine yourself being filled with the presence of the Lord, allowing His divine liveliness to permeate every aspect of your being. In this sacred space, ask the Lord to reveal what is possible in your relationships. Sit before Him with an open heart and mind, inviting Him to show you how to lean on Him and move in alignment with His love.

Release any painful patterns that stem from past traumas, surrendering them to the Lord's healing touch. Watch yourself hand each painful pattern to Him one by one. Imagine Him giving you, in exchange, new patterns rooted in love, hope, and faith. Let go of a suspicious or protective mindset and instead embrace the transformative power of love.

As He continues to pour into you, imagine a life overflowing with love, where you set healthy boundaries while nurturing deep connections. Imagine yourself speaking with gentleness, allowing love to flow through your words and actions. Envision the person you aspire to be in your relationships and the fulfillment you desire to receive. Notice that you have faith as He fills you.

Ask Him, "How can I create more goodness in my relationships. What does that look like to You?" Reflect on what He shows you.

Take a few moments to sit in silence, allowing His images and words to resonate within you. Remain open to any additional insights or guidance that the Lord may impart. When you are ready, gently bring your awareness back to the present moment, carrying with you the divine vision of God-filled relationships.

Use this QR code to access audible versions of activities.

INDIVIDUAL HEARTWORK – CHAPTER ELEVEN REVIEW

Reflect on and journal your answers to the below questions.

1. What was it like for you to write your purpose statement? What did you discover about yourself that was new insight?

2. How can you maintain momentum with walking in purpose?

3. What are the roadblocks to walking in purpose for which you need to watch out?

4. Is there something in this chapter that the Lord's been speaking to you, but you have not acted upon yet? How will you act upon what He is saying to you in obedience at this time?

5. What patterns are you determined to overcome in your relationships?

HEART GROUP DISCUSSION - TIME TO SHARE.

1. Share with your sisters your purpose statement. This might feel vulnerable, but it is important to share what God has put in you, He is not ashamed of you!

2. What was the hardest part of this chapter? What was the easiest part of this chapter?

3. Share with your sisters what impressed you most by the Spirit as you were working through this chapter.

4. Discuss with your sisters the importance of accountability in regard to fulfilling purpose.

5. Discuss with your sisters the importance of owning your side of the street in the creation of healthy relationships. Also, explore how when we are healthy, it brings out unhealthy behaviors from others at times and how to overcome it while walking in love.

Keystone Scriptures for Restoring My Purpose

NOW MEMORIZE THESE KEYSTONE SCRIPTURES:

For I know the plans I have for you," declares the Lord, "plans to prosper you and not to harm you, plans to give you hope and a future.

Jeremiah 29:11 (NIV)

You can make many plans, but the Lord's purpose will prevail.

Proverbs 19:21 (NLT)

For we are God's handiwork, created in Christ Jesus to do good works, which God prepared in advance for us to do.

Ephesians 2:10 (NIV)

LET US PRAY.

Lord, I pray that You would help us to incorporate everything we have learned on this journey and to move forward in purpose. Thank You for all the healing and for giving us the grace to become all You have made us to be.

In Jesus' name, Amen.

Chapter

T W E L V E

RESTORING MY LIFE

Wait and listen, everyone who is thirsty! Come to the waters; and he who has no money, come, buy and eat! Yes, come, buy [priceless, spiritual] wine and milk without money and without price [simply for the self-surrender that accepts the blessing].

Why do you spend your money for that which is not bread, and your earnings for what does not satisfy? Hearken diligently to Me, and eat what is good, and let your soul delight itself in fatness [the profuseness of spiritual joy].

Incline your ear [submit and consent to the divine will] and come to Me; hear, and your soul will revive; and I will make an everlasting covenant or league with you, even the sure mercy (kindness, goodwill, and compassion) promised to David.

Isaiah 55:1-3 (AMPC)

SUPPLIES

For this chapter's Heartwork, you will need a pen or pencil and your *Heart Journey*™ *Journal*.

INDIVIDUAL HEARTWORK – RESTORING MY LIFE

An activity I have found effective with my clients after they have gone through something momentous is to ask them to write twelve chapter titles that represent what they learned during that season with the title of the book being, *Everything I Need to Know, I Learned During [Momentous Event]*. This activity helps us pull out the best lessons from a considerable experience. For this activity, you will write twelve chapter titles of your own making, and describe through them the key life-changing insights you learned during your Heart Journey™. Make up your own chapter titles below and then describe each chapter title with a short summary.

Here is an example of two titles from Deborah:

Chapter 1 Title: I Deserve to Be Pursued

Chapter 2 Title: Avoidant People Are Not Good For Me

Now it is your turn:

Chapter 1 Title:

Summary:

Chapter 2 Title:

Summary:

Chapter 3 Title:

Summary:

Chapter 4 Title:

Summary:

Chapter 5 Title:

Summary:

Chapter 6 Title:

Summary:

Chapter 7 Title:

Summary:

Chapter 8 Title:

Summary:

Chapter 9 Title:

Summary:

Chapter 10 Title:

Summary:

Chapter 11 Title:

Summary:

Chapter 12 Title:

Summary:

Next, write a letter to Jesus thanking Him for all He did for you in this journey. He loves it when we come back and thank Him (Luke 17:11-19).

Lastly, write out your plan for continuing your healing journey.

And enjoy the scripted activities from our study at any time by submitting your best email here:

LET US PRAY.

Father, may we embrace the beauty that arises from the depths of suffering, just as salvation emerged from the ultimate trauma. May we trust in God's meticulous plan, knowing that He weaves together every pain and wound into a tapestry of immeasurable good. And may we seek continual encounters with Jesus, being filled with the Holy Spirit, as we embark on Your journey of restoration and purpose.

In Jesus' name, Amen.

Keystone Scriptures for Restoring My Life

NOW MEMORIZE THESE KEYSTONE SCRIPTURES:

It was granted her to clothe herself with fine linen, bright and pure"— for the fine linen is the righteous deeds of the saints.

Revelation 19:8 (ESV)

Christ redeemed us from the curse of the law by becoming a curse for us—for it is written, "Cursed is everyone who is hanged on a tree"—

Galatians 3:13 (ESV)

The Spirit of the Lord God is upon me,
Because the Lord has anointed and commissioned me
To bring good news to the humble and afflicted;
He has sent me to bind up [the wounds of] the brokenhearted,
To proclaim release [from confinement and condemnation] to the [physical and spiritual] captives and freedom to prisoners,
To proclaim the favorable year of the Lord,
And the day of vengeance and retribution of our God,
To comfort all who mourn,
To grant to those who mourn in Zion the following:
To give them a turban instead of dust [on their heads, a sign of mourning],
The oil of joy instead of mourning,
The garment [expressive] of praise instead of a disheartened spirit.
So they will be called the trees of righteousness [strong and magnificent, distinguished for integrity, justice, and right standing with God],
The planting of the Lord, that He may be glorified.

Restoring My Life

Then they will rebuild the ancient ruins,
They will raise up and restore the former desolations;
And they will renew the ruined cities,
The desolations (deserted settlements) of many generations.

Isiah 61:1-4 (AMP)

References

[1] Christian persecution higher than ever as Open Doors' World Watch List marks 30 years." Religion News. January 17, 2023. Retrieved from https://religionnews.com/2023/01/17/christian-persecution-higher-than-ever-as-opendoors-world-watch-list-marks-30-years/

[2] Miller, W. R., & Delaney, H. D. (Eds.). (2005). Judeo-Christian perspectives on psychology: Human nature, motivation, and change. American Psychological Association. https://doi.org/10.1037/10859-000

[3] Netburn, D. (2023, January 9). Group therapy from the pulpit? How a professor and minister is changing psychology. Los Angeles Times. Retrieved from hIps://www.la'mes.com/california/story/2023-01-09/psychologistand-minister-thema-bryant.

[4] Pearson, J., Naselaris, T., Holmes, E. A., & Kosslyn, S. M. (2015). Mental Imagery: Functional Mechanisms and Clinical Applications. Trends in Cognitive Sciences, 19(10), 590-602. doi: 10.1016/j.tics.2015.08.003